COTTESMORE   SCHOOL

FORM   PRIZE

<u>VI</u>

AWARDED   TO

ROBERT CRAWFORD

Easter 1986

SOPWITH CAMEL
KING OF COMBAT

by

CHAZ BOWYER

'Here was a buzzing hornet, a wild thing, burning the air like raw spirit fires the throat.'
. . . N. Macmillan, INTO THE BLUE.

FATHER OF ALL CAMELS. The first, unserialled prototype F.1 at Booklands in late December 1916. Note one-piece upper wing; sloping guns' hump; and lack of 'centre-section' cut-out in upper wing. The lower wing dihedral — a recognition point on all Camels — is evident in the second view.

CONTENTS

©1978 Chaz Bowyer

ISBN 0 9502825 7X

Produced by Oxford Publishing Co.
Set by Gem Graphic Services, Didcot, Oxon.
Bound by Kemp Hall Bindery, Oxford.
Printed by B.H. Blackwell in the City of Oxford.

Published by
G L A S N E Y   P R E S S
Falmouth

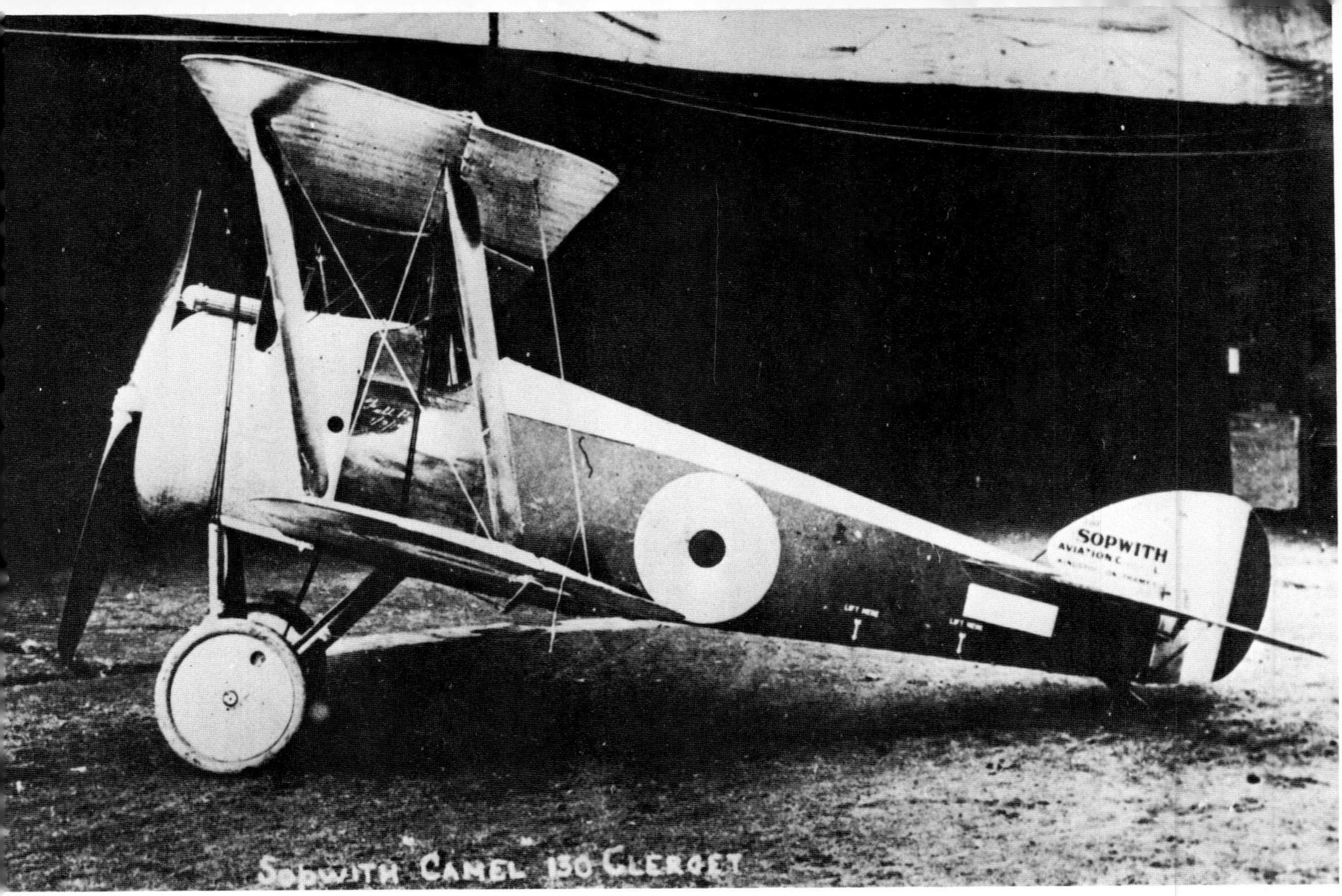

Sopwith Camel 130 Clerget

The first prototype fitted with a 130hp
Clerget engine, and incorporating a small,
apparently ovular cut-out section in the upper
wing; possibly for compensation for the small
rudder.

The first prototype, still with one-piece upper
wing and sloping gun fairing, but with rect-
angular cut-out in upper wing.

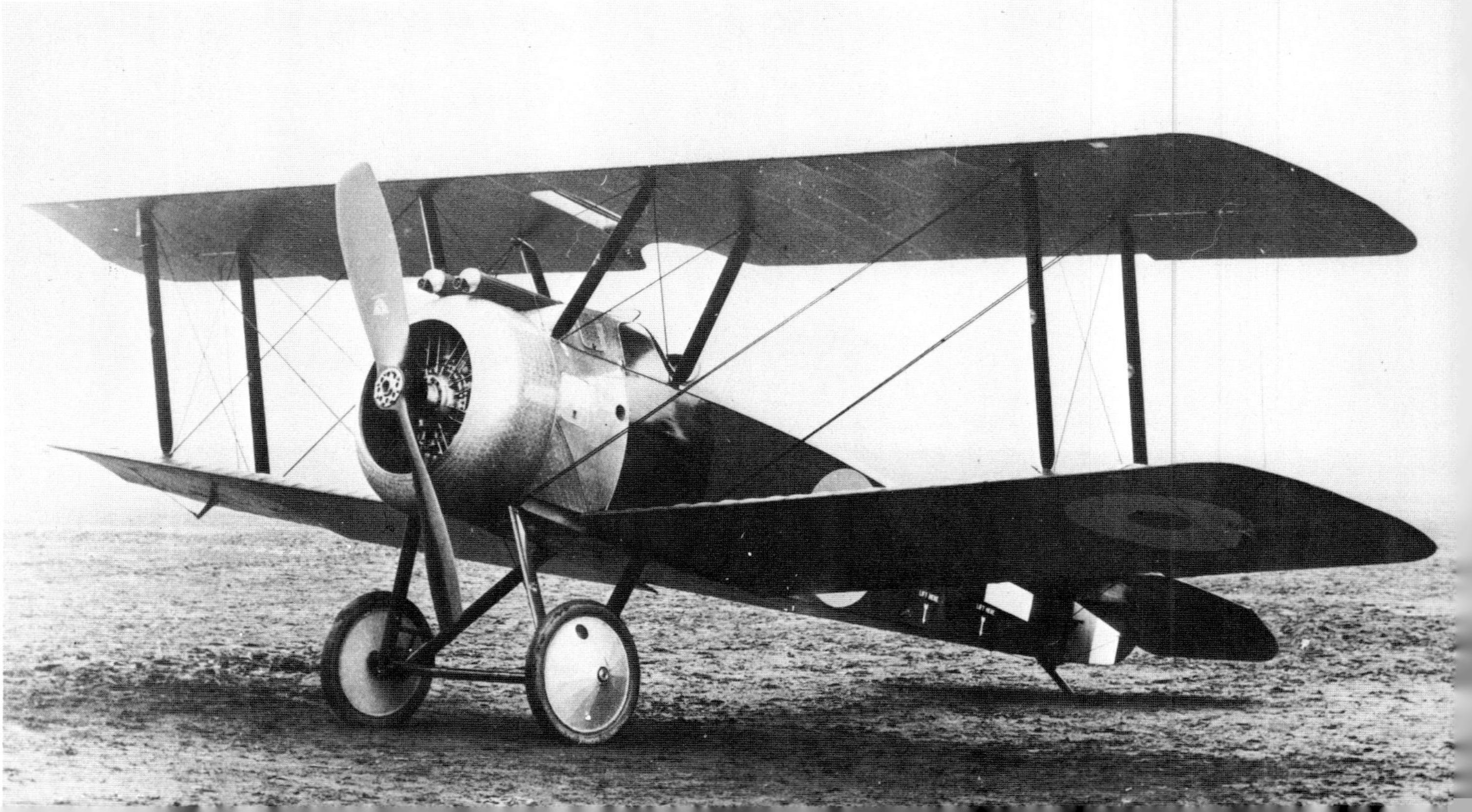

INTRODUCTION

It is indicative of the international fame of the Sopwith Camel, and its pre-eminence in aviation history, that even today, sixty years after that stubby little fighter was in its heyday, its name remains synonymous with the world's first aerial struggle in 1914-18. A pug-nosed, wilful biplane which was almost equally lauded or vilified by the men who flew it, the Camel emerged from that conflict as the most successful aerial combatant; having accounted for more of its opponents than any other single aircraft type of any nation participating in the war.

Yet the original design for the Camel was no isolated spark of genius but a logical development of existing ideas and requirements. In an era when aeroplane design was imperfectly understood, and the essential needs for aerial combat empirical, the Camel's stumpy concentration of essential facets provided a near-ideal fighting machine which, in intelligent hands, could outwit and out-manoeuvre virtually any opponent. Undoubtedly, the Camel was the nearest approach to an ideal aerobatic machine ever produced for fighting duties during World War One. It could be looped under perfect control from a low air speed, and flick-rolled safely at grass-cutting height without danger of height loss. Its greatest combat characteristic was an ability to make a turn to left or right in mere seconds, again without loss of precious height. Due to the concentration of all greater weight masses centrally, combined with the significant torque reaction from its rotary engine, a Camel could 'turn on a sixpence' (in the contemporary vernacular), and a Camel pilot could reverse his flight path within less than twice the length of its fuselage — or so it was claimed.

Paradoxically, it was this facet which earned for the Camel the title 'Hun-killer' — the reference being in contemporary airmen's slang where the term 'Hun' was applied generically — and dispassionately — to all student pilots and enemy airmen alike. Unless the lighting turn was handled intelligently a Camel's nose would drop swiftly. The immediate resulting spin was rapid and, usually, fatal to the pilot if insufficient height was in hand. Designed solely for combat, the Camel was no suitable vehicle for the beginner, being mercilessly unforgiving of careless control, and remorseless in punishing any hesitation on the part of a pilot. Once its idiosyncrasies were properly understood, however, the Camel offered the fighting pilot a weapon of war which could and usually did hold its own against all opposition. An analysis of all Camel losses known in the combat areas shows that a majority occurred with relatively inexperienced pilots flying the early, and therefore most dangerous, sorties of their brief operational careers.

With all its fighting advantages, the Camel lacked a high speed and fast rate of climb when compared with the later German Albatros and Fokker fighters of 1918. Indeed, it has been frequently asserted by ex-Camel pilots that once committed to combat a Camel had little choice but to fight its way home — hence the unrivalled tally of opponents destroyed or brought down; but as one distinguished Camel pilot put it succinctly, 'That was, after all, the object of the exercise. . .' A Camel's best fighting ceiling was around 12,000 feet, and given such conditions its pilot could confidently take on all-comers.

SOPWITH CAMEL - 110 H.P. CLERGET - TYPE F.1.

2nd MACHINE

1917.

S.121

In this rear view of the so-termed '2nd Machine', the upper wing is in three distinct pieces, including a wide centre-section. Possibly the reference (inscribed on the original Sopwith negative) refers to the second production machine.

Despite its fame few truly accurate accounts of the Sopwith Camel and its many variants have been published since 1918, although an excess of repeated legends have continued to blur the true story of the Camel's exploits. Two exceptions to this mountain of misinformation have been the original and exhaustive studies made by J M Bruce, MA, FRHistS, AMRAeS, and Bruce Robertson. For the sake of simplicity of narrative, and in deference to the existing and readily-available technical information sources on the Camels by these two researcher-authors, my own text is aimed deliberately at presenting the more general operational history of the Camels, their pilots and deeds. Much, though by no means all, purely technical data in this book is based on the original findings and reasoned conclusions of those researchers; although ultimate responsibility for any misinterpretations remains entirely mine. My debt to both men, who gave unstinted help and valued service, is heavy.

A note of explanation is perhaps necessary to amplify the various tabulations of high-scoring Camels and pilots in the appropriate appendices. Each has been verified by scrupulous examination and multiple cross-checking of contemporary records, documents, personal log books et al. The bulk of this research was cheerfully undertaken on my behalf by Norman L R Franks, whose deep friendship I strained to the limit by constant queries, and whose voluminous personal records — the result of many years of meticulous research — were made freely available to me without demur. The whole question of fighter pilots' 'victories' requires a book to itself, but a brief word here might not be amiss concerning these particular appendices. Under the contemporary official rulings in World War One, any pilot claiming a combat 'victory' was required to thoroughly satisfy certain conditions before any such claim was officially sanctioned. Although those conditions varied throughout the war, and indeed varied widely between the separate Allied air Services; in the main they required independent 'confirmation' by witnesses, air or ground. It should be clearly stated that all 'confirmed victories' were by no means conclusive. In general, an enemy aircraft was only claimed as 'destroyed' where positive evidence was available, such as wreckage or a burning aircraft seen by other pilots — though even in the latter case there are authenticated instances of men surviving in burned machines — or similar justifiable 'proof.' Too many aviation 'historians' have in the past equated 'victories' with aircraft actually destroyed; whereas in fact the bulk of 'victories' claimed by pilots of all air Services during 1914-18 came in the official category 'Out of Control'. This last category applied generically to any aircraft sent down, apparently thoroughly defeated, but whose ultimate fate was not actually witnessed.

For many items of authentic information and data relating to the Camels' history I am deeply indebted to the almost embarrassing generosity of a host of good friends and acquaintances. To list them all here would be tedious to the reader, and possibly pretentious on my part. Nevertheless I would like each to know that their selfless generosity is by no means forgotten. In particular, the credit for the somewhat massive accumulation of photographs gathered during many years of research for this history is certainly not mine alone. Many friends (listed separately) gave me a literal *carte blanche* to use photos from their own hardily-won collections. With such a profusion of possible illustrations my aim has been to present a final selection which will to a great degree supplement the many well-used, even hackneyed, Camel photographs published in the past; yet still offer a 'whole' photographic record of the aircraft and their crews. Perhaps inevitably a number herein though familiar to the avid historian have had to be repeated, being the only ones known to illustrate a specific subject or because they are the best available for pure pictorial value. Occasionally a photograph is (apparently) the only one ever taken of a particular subject.

Chaz Bowyer

Norwich, 1977

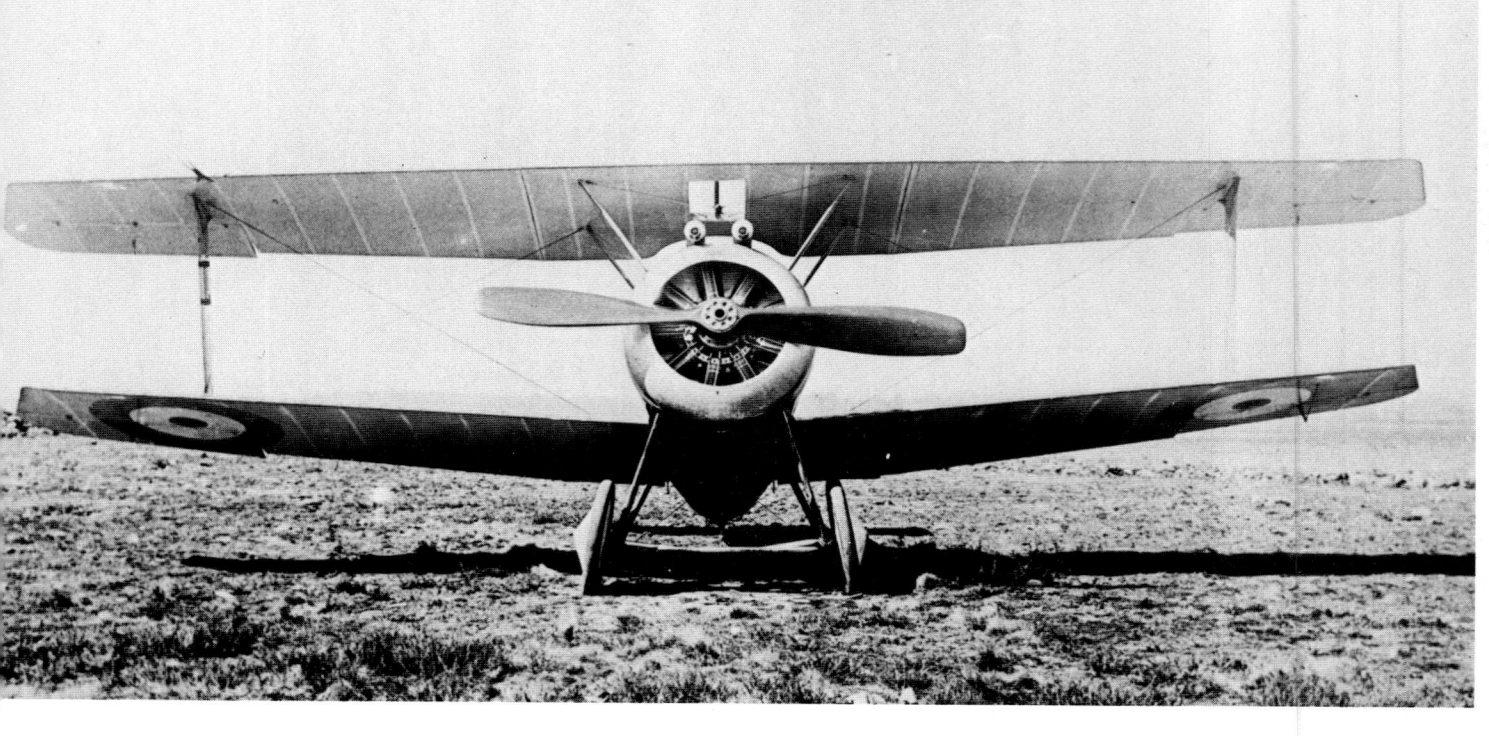

Two views of the Sopwith F.1/1, 'Taper-Wing' Camel in early 1917. The single 'plank' inter-plane struts and sharply tapered wings are self-evident. Note also the widened under-carriage Vee-strutting.

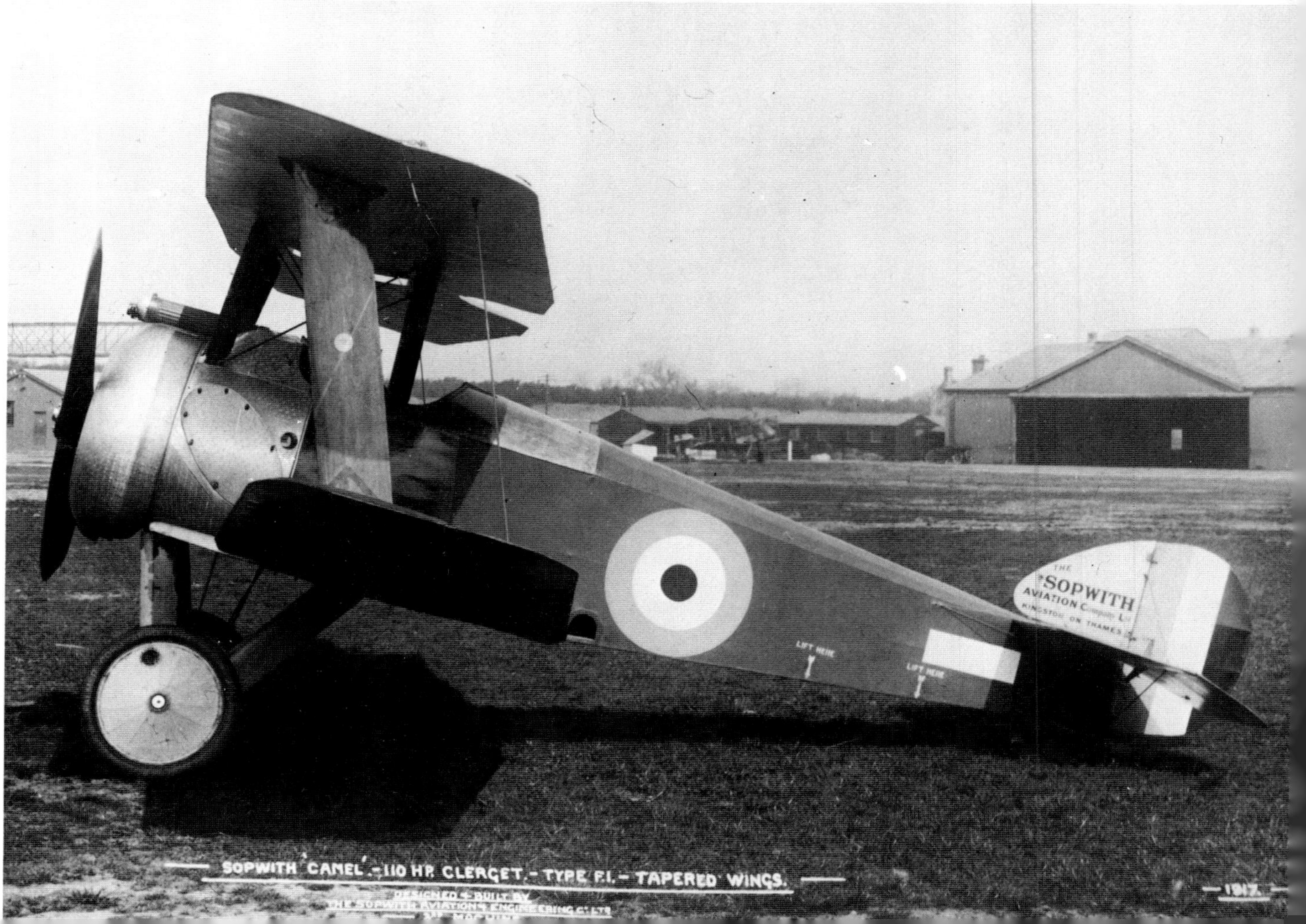
THE SOPWITH AVIATION Company Ltd KINGSTON ON THAMES
LIFT HERE
LIFT HERE
SOPWITH 'CAMEL'.- 110 HP. CLERGET. - TYPE F.I. - TAPERED WINGS.
DESIGNED & BUILT BY
THE SOPWITH AVIATION & ENGINEERING Co LTD
1917.

GLOSSARY OF ABBREVIATIONS

AAFS	—	Advanced Air Fighting School
AAP	—	Aircraft Acceptance Park
AEF	—	American Expeditionary Force
AFC	—	Australian Flying Corps (See also, Decorations)
ARD	—	Aeroplane Repair Depot
BEF	—	British Expeditionary Force
CFS	—	Central Flying School (Upavon)
CTD	—	Central Transit Depot
EA	—	Enemy Aircraft
Flik	—	Fliegerkompagnie (Austro-Hungarian equivalent of RAF squadron)
Flt	—	Flight (sub-formation of Squadron)
HD	—	Home Defence (United Kingdom)
IF	—	Independent Force (Royal Air Force)
Jasta	—	Jagdstaffel (German counterpart to RFC/RAF squadron)
NFTS	—	Night Flying Training Squadron
OP	—	Offensive Patrol
RAF	—	Royal Aircraft Factory, Farnborough (before April 1st, 1918)
RAF	—	Royal Air Force (from April 1st 1918)
RFC	—	Royal Flying Corps
RNAS	—	Royal Naval Air Service
R/T	—	Radio Telephony
S of AF	—	School of Air Fighting
S of SF	—	School of Special Flying (Gosport)
SOC	—	Struck Off Charge
Sqn	—	Squadron (RFC/RNAS/RAF)
TDS	—	Training Depot Station
TS	—	Training Squadron
USAS	—	United States Air Service (Army)
USN	—	United States Navy
W/T	—	Wireless Telegraphy

Ranks British:

2/Lt	—	Second Lieutenant
Lt	—	Lieutenant
Capt	—	Captain
Maj	—	Major
Lt-Col	—	Lieutenant-Colonel
FSLt	—	Flight Sub-Lieutenant (RNAS)
F/Lt	—	Flight Lieutenant (RNAS)
F/Cdr	—	Flight Commander (RNAS)
S/Cdr	—	Squadron Commander (RNAS)

Ranks, German:

Fl	—	Flieger (Private)
Gef	—	Gefreiter (Private, 1st Class)
Unteroff	—	Unteroffizier (Corporal)
Vzfwbl	—	Vizefeldwebel (Sergeant)
Offstvtr	—	Offizier-stell-vertreter (Acting officer)
Ltn	—	Leutnant (Second Lieutenant)
Obltn	—	Oberleutnant (First Lieutenant)
Haupt	—	Hauptmann (Captain, Army infantry)
Rittm	—	Rittmeister (Captain, Army cavalry)

Decorations, British:

AFC	—	Air Force Cross
DFC	—	Distinguished Flying Cross
DSC	—	Distinguished Service Cross (Navy only)
DSO	—	Distinguished Service Order
MC	—	Military Cross (Army only)
VC	—	Victoria Cross (Supreme British award)

F.1 Camel, N6332, a Sopwith-built machine which served with 70 Squadron RFC, and was lost in action on July 18th, 1917.

B3751, the first F.1 Camel to be issued to the RFC. Tested extensively at Martlesham Heath from June 1917 to January 1918, it was allotted for Home Defence duties during this period.

ORIGINS

By the late summer of 1916 the steadily increasing tempo of aerial fighting over the Western Front in France had created an obvious and vital need for aircraft designers of all nations to produce aircraft specifically fashioned for pure fighting roles. Germany already had such an aircraft, the Fokker E.1 *Eindecker* (monoplane); a single-seat, nimble fighter, fitted with a fixed machine gun firing forward through the propeller arc, which already held a form of aerial supremacy above the battlefields. Such British single-seaters as did exist, like the De Havilland 2 and Sopwith Pup, quickly proved their superior qualities to the Fokker, but the further introduction in August 1916 of the German *jagdstaffeln* (literally, 'hunting squadrons') equipped with early versions of the Albatros D and Halberstadt D scouts, each armed with twin synchronised machine guns, soon regained air superiority for Germany. At that period in Britain three major fighter designs were already taking final shape which were to have a significant impact on the aerial struggle in the following years. At the Royal Aircraft Factory, Farnborough, the SE5 was almost ready; while further west the two-seat Bristol F2a was about to be produced for the Royal Flying Corps. Later, as the F2b, this latter design was to earn, deservedly, the unofficial title 'King of Two-Seaters'. Third of those significant designs was the Sopwith F.1, soon to achieve undying fame as the 'Camel'.

Designed by the Sopwith team of T.O.M. Sopwith, F. Sigrist, H. Hawker, with R.J. Ashfield and Herbert Smith deserving the greater measure of recognition for their parts in the initial lay-out design; the F.1. was the latest in an already long line of highly successful Sopwith aircraft, following after the Tabloid, Pup and Triplane. On December 22nd, 1916 the first prototype Sopwith F.1 was passed out of Sopwith's Experimental Department, having satisfied all ground acceptance tests. It was by no means a beautiful aeroplane. Compact and snub-nosed, the little biplane seemed to exude an air of sheer aggressiveness, and was simply a highly functional design. It had been originated as a fighter and its appearance fitted the conception superbly. In construction the F.1 was in no way unusual for its period. The fuselage was a conventional wooden box-girder, wire-braced assembly, with a gently-rounded top decking stretching from the cockpit to the tail. The cockpit sides were ply-covered, whilst the forward engine bay was panelled in sheet aluminium. With the exceptions of the engine compartment and the cockpit, the remainder of the fuselage was fabric-covered. Wings and tail assemblies were of the contemporary pattern of fabric-skinned wooden structure. The first, un-serialled F.1 prototype differed in several ways from eventual production machines. Primarily, the upper wing was built as a one-piece assembly, with only a small trailing edge cut-out for pilot vision upwards. The equivalent of a centre-section area was wide, extending beyond the centre-section struts; whilst wing ailerons were relatively short, spanning only from the wing tips to the spruce interplane main struts. In front of the cockpit were two Vickers .303 machine guns, side by side in what was to become the standard armament arrangement for nearly 20 years on most fighter aircraft of the world. The guns were housed partly in a 'hump' fairing which sloped upwards from the nose to the front rim of the cockpit. This sloping decking was originally considered as sufficient to protect the pilot's forward vision from slipstream effect and therefore no conventional wind-screen was fitted. Power for the first F.1 prototype came from a 110 hp Clerget 9Z rotary engine.

The most significant aspect of the new fighter was its concentration of all greater masses within a small section of the fuselage. Engine, guns, controls and pilot were tightly located within a mere seven feet length of fuselage — a factor which contributed greatly to the astonishing manoeuvrability of the F.1 and its later variants. Of historical significance was its armament arrangement of twin, side-by-side, forward-firing machine guns. The Sopwith F.1 was the first British fighter designed from the outset to employ this classic form of gun installation. A pronounced recognition aspect of the F.1 lay in its wing arrangement. The upper plane had no dihedral, although original ideas by the Sopwith team had envisaged a modest dihedral angle. In contrast, the lower wings were canted upwards from the fuselage at a five-degrees' angle of dihedral. It was a feature almost unique to the F.1 and could be recognised at extremely long range in the air. In overall appearance the F.1 offered an aura of pugnacity, likened by one pilot to that of a boxer dog, where the lean flanks give added importance to the hunched muscle-power of the shoulders and compact head.

Initial flying tests quickly established the F.1's most notable characteristic — its manoeuvrability. A combination of the rotary engine's torque qualities and the built-in masses' concentration centrally gave the F.1 turning capabilities unmatched by any previous design. Controls were highly sensitive and responded instantly to a pilot's lightest touch, giving the illusion that the aircraft virtually 'thought' of the next movement of its controls as fast as its master. It was a feature warmly welcomed by later pilots in the fighting zones, but one which betokened potential disaster for any student pilot unfamiliar with such rapid responses in any aircraft handled previously.

B3850, a Sopwith-built F.1 Camel fitted with a 100hp Gnome Monosoupape engine, trestled into flying attitude. Its 'presentation' name was LEPOQO; the first of three Camels so-titled in the event. This machine was struck off charge on August 29th, 1917.

B4612, built by Portholme, which was issued to 54 Squadron, and shot down intact in German lines on July 15th, 1918.

Just after Christmas Day, 1916 the first F.1 was given its initial air test by the celebrated Harry Hawker, who took off from Brooklands airfield and 'bounced into the air', to quote a contemporary witness. Hawker's after-flight report was enthusiastic and gave emphasis to the sensitivity of the controls. Further testing continued during January and February 1917, and three more 'prototypes' were quickly produced by the Sopwith firm. The first of these, titled F.1/1 but without a serial number, was also known as the Taper Wing. It was an attempt to simplify the basic F.1 wing and strut arrangement with a hope of improved performance. The wings of the F.1/1 tapered from a centre-section chord of five feet (six inches more than the F.1) to a wing-tip chord of three feet and six inches. Other differences to the first F.1 included an additional centre-section aperture cut-out, and a horizontal Vickers guns' hump fairing in place of the former sloping enclosure. With the decreased chord of the outer wings, conventional twin interplane struts were replaced by single, plank I-struts. Powered by a 130 hp Clerget 9B rotary, the F.1/1 was tested by the RFC Testing Squadron at Martlesham Heath in May 1917 but proved to be little improved in performance on the F.1, and had a rather faster landing speed. Additionally its taper wings presented slight complications from a production viewpoint and consequently the 'Taper Wing' was not considered for further development. In view of that decision, however, it is surprising to note that in December 1917 the Air Board discussed a proposal to build a '4F.1 Taper Wing Camel', and Contract A.S. 34594 was actually issued for the construction of four 'prototypes'. In the event these were never built.

A more direct descendant of the F.1 was the F.1/2 — believed to be the Naval prototype serialled N517, though documentary confirmation of this has so far eluded discovery. It differed little from the first F.1, but had the additional centre-section aperture, horizontal guns' hump fairing, and was fitted with a small windscreen in front of the cockpit. The side cowling was faired elliptically into the fuselage. First flown at Brooklands on February 26th, 1917, the F.1/2 was tested before being sent to the Royal Naval Air Service (RNAS) station at Dunkirk by March 1st. In the following six months N517 had a chequered career. By May 17th it was with 9 (N) Squadron undergoing Service evaluation; then moved to 11(N) Squadron briefly. On June 6th Flight Sub-Lieutenant S.T. Edwards flew comparative tests with a Nieuport single-seater. By June 14th it had moved to 12 (N) Squadron, where it suffered some damage on June 29th; and was finally wrecked at Dunkirk on August 20th, 1917, and 'deleted' from RNAS charge the following day.

The final un-serialled 'prototype' was designated F.1/3 and was delivered for testing at Martlesham Heath on March 24th, 1917, powered originally with a 130 hp Clerget 9B rotary engine. Later it was tested with at least two other types of rotary; a 110 hp Le Rhone 9J, and an experimental Clerget LS (Long Stroke) — this latter being later retitled as a 140 hp Clerget 9Bf. The F.1/3 retained the one-piece upper wing and short ailerons of the first prototype, but was for all intents and purposes the model for future production F.1's. From available evidence it would appear that the F.1/3 was the first prototype to be 'christened' with the unlikely soubriquet 'Camel'. Sir Henry Tizard, an RFC technical officer at the time of the F.1/3's arrival at Martlesham Heath, has recorded that one of the Testing Squadron's pilots on seeing the stubby little newcomer remarked, 'Just to look at the beast gives me the hump at the thought of flying it!' If indeed this was the origin of the name Camel, the nickname must have been spread quickly because references to Camels as such were evident in several contemporary accounts of the early part of 1917. As with its beloved predecessor the Sopwith 'Pup', the nickname was never officially adopted, but became firmly established by constant usage by pilots who flew F.1's.

In May 1917 a second Naval prototype, serialled N518, was tested at Martlesham Heath and was of particular interest in that it was the first to use a new type of rotary engine, the AR1 (Admiralty Rotary No. 1) of 150 hp, designed by Wilfred Owen Bentley, an RNAS engineering liaison officer. The AR1 — soon to be retitled BR1 (Bentley Rotary No. 1) — was virtually a Clerget, but with steel-lined aluminium cylinders. Tests in N518 soon established its superiority over similar conventional Clergets and, indeed, BR1-engined F.1's were the first to be issued for operations in France, as detailed in a later chapter. Meanwhile the first production batch of F.1's had been ordered from the parent Sopwith company to a Naval requirement — serials N6330—N6379 inc. — and deliveries commenced on May 7th, 1917. A further batch of 250 F.1's (initially) was sub-contracted out to the Lincoln firm of Ruston Proctor on May 22nd (Contract AS 1809). In its production form the F.1 replaced the prototype's one-piece upper wing with a three-piece structure, but in most respects was based on the F.1/3. Two further prototypes and a proposed floatplane version of the Camel were produced in the early weeks of 1917. Known officially as Sopwith 2F.1 'Ships Camels' these were designed specially for use with the naval arm, and their history and operational use are detailed in a further chapter for clarity.

B6422, an F.1 tested at Martlesham Heath between December 1917 and February 1918.

B6251, one of the early F.1 Camels issued to 70 Squadron RFC, the first RFC Camel unit. This machine later saw service with 28 Squadron.

WESTERN FRONT

With full production of F.1 Camels gaining momentum, the first examples were issued to operational units in France; the first recipients being the naval pilots of 4 (N) Squadron, based at Dunkirk. The date of the first operational F.1's arrival continues to elude confirmation, but it is known that F.1's N6337, N6345, N6347 and N6363 were on 4 (N) Squadron's strength during the first week of June 1917. The new fighters were welcomed by the squadron, whose existing aircraft, Sopwith Pups, though delightful to fly, had proved only moderately successful in intercepting the early Gotha raiders attacking Britain at that period — Dunkirk being situated directly in the flight path of the German bombers en route to England. The first-ever recorded Camel combat took place on June 4th, 1917 when Flight Commander Alexander M Shook of 4 (N) Squadron, in N6347, attacked an enemy aircraft 15 miles off Nieuport. The German dived steeply away and disappeared in the dense sea haze east of Middlekerke. On the following day Shook, again in N6347, sighted 15 enemy aircraft between Nieuport and Ostende and promptly attacked. His fire sent one scout down to crash on a beach, while a second German scout was later claimed as out of control. The Camel was truly 'blooded'. On June 25th Flight Sub-Lieutenant Chadwick in N6345, and Shook in N6363, tackled a mixed formation of German two-seaters and scouts. In the ensuing combat Chadwick destroyed one two-seater in flames.

The Camels' first encounters with the giant Gotha bombers occurred early in the morning of July 4th, when a five-Camel formation from 4 (N) Squadron met a loose gaggle of sixteen Gothas about 30 miles north-west of Ostende at heights varying between 12 and 15,000 feet. Alexander Shook (N6363) attacked one Gotha which dived away steeply pluming black smoke. Switching to a second Gotha, Shook continued firing until his guns jammed. In N6337 Flight Sub-Lieutenant S.E. Ellis dived into the centre of the bombers and fired some 300 rounds into one Gotha which stalled and then fell away erratically, issuing brown smoke from the area around its rear gunner's cockpit. A third Camel pilot, Flight Sub-Lieutenant, A.J. Enstone, claimed one Gotha as damaged, and a second bomber as forced down low over neutral Dutch soil. These 'victories', claimed in all good faith on available evidence, resulted in the award to Shook of a Distinguished Service Cross (DSC); though post-1918 examination of German records revealed that no German losses were incurred by these Camel attacks. Tragically, one of those pioneer Camel pilots, S.E. Ellis, also became the first-known Camel casualty when, on July 12th in N6337, he spun into the ground during a routine flight.*

Re-equipment of operational fighter units in France was quickly implemented. The second naval unit to receive the type was 6 (N) Squadron in July 1917, and by the end of that month six other squadrons had begun to exchange their previous equipment. No. 9 (N) Squadron received its first Camel on July 13th, and by August 4th had completed the exchange for its former Sopwith Triplanes; while two other naval fighter units, 8 (N) and 10 (N) Squadrons completed re-equipment by September. The first RFC unit to receive Camels was a former Sopwith 1½ Strutter squadron, 70, based at Fienvillers in June 1917. 70 Squadron wasted little time in testing their new fighters in action, and on June 27th Captain Clive Collett in B3756 scored the squadron's first Camel victory. Later this particular Camel was to claim at least five more victories in the capable hands of another 70 Squadron pilot, Captain N.W. Webb, MC. In July 45 Squadron also commenced exchanging their well-worn Sopwith 1½ Strutters for Camels. No. 6 (N) Squadron's existence as a single-seater unit ended somewhat abruptly on August 26th, 1917 prior to its eventual reformation as a bomber unit at the end of the year; but in September four more Camel units were newly equipped. No. 3 Squadron RFC began re-equipment in that month, while 28 Squadron at Yatesbury, Wiltshire was fully equipped by early October and flew as a complete Camel unit to St Omer, France on October 8th; taking up residence at Droglandt airfield later that day. Yet another former Sopwith 1½ Strutter unit of the RFC to change to Camels was 43 Squadron at Auchel, which flew its first Camel operations on September 5th. The fourth unit to become Camel-equipped in September 1917 was the RNAS 'Seaplane Defence Squadron' at St Pol, which exchanged its Sopwith Pups, and on January 15th, 1918 was officially retitled as 13 (N) Squadron, RNAS.

---

* This refers only to casualties *caused* by a Camel. In fact FSL L F W Smith of 4(N) Squadron was killed *in action* on June 13th, 1917, in Camel N6362; and FSL E W Busby of 4(N) was killed *in action* on July 10th, 1917 in Camel N6361.

15

Fourteen Camels of 8(N) Squadron 'on the line' at Mont St Eloi, circa January 1918. The nearest F.1, B6340, 'P' was usually flown by Flight Commander Robert J O Compston, who gained nine of his victories in this machine. It also saw service (previously) with 6(N) Squadron, and by July 1918 was in use as a trainer at 50 TDS, Eastbourne. The tiny propeller boss spinner was a local modification, not uncommon on Camel units. (Above)

Flight Lieutenant Alexander M Shook, RNAS of 4(N) Squadron, first Camel pilot to claim a combat victory. (Left)

F.1 Camels of 9(N) Squadron, bearing colourful individual markings in place of fuselage roundels. In foreground is B3905, named MURYEL, which later served with 12(N) Squadron in early 1918. At right is the Camel usually flown by Flight Lieutenant Francis J W Mellersh (possibly B7245?). (Below)

Camels of 210 Squadron RAF at Teteghem, mid-1918, bearing the unit's post-March 1918 insignia of a white circle. Nearest, 'S', was F5914, a rebuilt Camel which served with 201 Squadron prior to joining 210; with which latter unit it was lost in action on July 22nd, 1918 (Lt H T Mellings). Behind it, B7153, 'X' was variously piloted by Captain L P Coombes, Lts I C Sanderson, and S C Joseph.

A Ruston, Proctor-built F.1, B2361, 'C' of 70 Squadron which was shot down behind German lines on October 27th, 1917 by Leutnant Jacobs of Jagd-staffel 7.

No. 3 Squadron Camel line-up at Inchy, 1918. This unit first received Camels in September 1917.

Pilots accustomed to the docile Pup or tractable 1½ Strutters soon came to recognise the fighting potential of the fierce little Camel and exploited the aircraft's fire-power and sharp manoeuvrability to good advantage. Some of the early Camel combats were with the notorious *Jagdstaffel* 11, led by Germany's eventual 'Ace of aces', Manfred von Richthofen, and on July 20th a Camel of 70 Squadron became the sixth claimed victory of Vizefeldwebel Kurt Wüsthoff of that unit. Six days later, however, Leutnant Otto Brauneck, a nine-victory veteran of *Jasta* 11 was killed in combat with 70 Squadron's Camels. On the ground the third battle of Ypres commenced at dawn on July 31st, 1917 and was to continue until November 10th. During that period the British armies forced their way through the German defences and captured Passchendaele Ridge, but the main objective of the offensive — to roll up the German right flank — failed due to atrocious wet weather conditions. Aircraft of the RFC and RNAS were used extensively in a low-level role, ground-strafing and bombing at tree-top height; and the Camel units became a spearhead of this highly dangerous mode of operations. Fitted with racks under their fuselages to carry four 20/25 lb Cooper bombs, the low-flying Camels soon became adept as bombers, yet retained their mounting reputation as excellent dogfighters. On September 3rd, for example, various patrols from 45 Squadron accounted for at least six German scouts during the course of the day, including one by Captain Arthur Harris, who in World War Two was to direct the fortunes of RAF Bomber Command for three years.

On September 15th the relatively-new Camel met the first example of its nearest rival for the title of the war's greatest dogfighter, when a patrol of 10 (N) Squadron Camels surprised a lone Fokker Dr. 1 Triplane near Wervicq. The Dr. 1 was the second production triplane, Fl. 102/17 and was being flown by the noted 33-victory 'ace' Oberleutnant Kurt Wolff, commander of *Jagdstaffel* 11 of the recently-formed *Richthofen Jagdgeschwader* — known to the Allied airmen as the 'Circus'. Wolff had set out with a patrol of four Albatros scouts but temporarily lost contact with his formation. Before his men could hasten to his aid, Wolff was attacked by the leading 10 (N) Squadron Camel, B3833, piloted by Flight Sub-Lieutenant N.M. MacGregor, whose fire damaged the triplane's engine. The Fokker fell away, burst into flames, and then exploded. Four days after Wolff's death came the first organised Camel bombing operations when aircraft from 70 and 10 (N) Squadrons were despatched to strafe German troop positions all along the Ypres front. One of the 70 Squadron pilots involved in these operations was Second Lieutenant F.G. Quigley, a Canadian, who was eventually to achieve a credited victory tally of 34 enemy aircraft — all in Camels of 70 Squadron.

As the ground struggle raged on into October, fresh Camel units came into being. At Wye, in Kent, 65 Squadron was brought to full strength with new Camels and flew to France on October 24th to join the war, being based initially at La Lovie. Meanwhile 3 Squadron RFC flew its first Camel operations on October 6th; and 66 Squadron started to receive Camels to replace their battleworn Sopwith Pups. A veteran Sopwith Triplane unit, 1 (N) Squadron ceased to be attached to the RFC on November 2nd, 1917 and was withdrawn to Dover, England for a rest and re-equipment with Camels, with effect from December 10th. The 'rest' period was interrupted on at least three occasions when pilots were hastily sent up to intercept German bombers heading for London, but on February 14th, 1918, commanded by the doughty Major Roderic Dallas, an Australian, 1 (N) Squadron, fully equipped with Camels, flew to France and settled in to Teteghem airfield, ready for further operations. On November 7th, 1917 another Sopwith Pup unit, 46 Squadron RFC based at Le Hameau, received the first of its eventual full establishment of Camels. Despite the urgency of the Ypres operations, the situation on the Italian front at this time necessitated immediate Allied support for the crumbling Italian forces. One part of that aid included the transfer of three Camel units to Italy. Accordingly, Nos 28, 45 and 66 Squadrons were withdrawn from France during November-December 1917; their Camels and personnel being despatched by rail and road to the new theatre of operations.

Another 3 Squadron Camel, with its pilot Lt Rogers. Note widened upper wing centre-section cut-out for better visibility, and 'cooling' slots in the engine lower cowling. Just visible in left background is a wing-less Handley Page 0/400 bomber fuselage.

C Flight, 43 Squadron's Camels at Touquin, July 1918. Nearest is D6402, 'S', the personal steed of Captain Henry W Woollett, DSO, MC, in which he scored at least 17 combat victories, including his famous six-in-a-day feat. It bears (unusually) extra cockades on the upper surface of the lower wings. Behind, D1785, 'Z', had previously served with 73 Squadron. 43 Squadron's unit insignia—two sloping white bars, one each side of the fuselage cockade—were repeated above the upper wing.

NAVAL CIRCUS. Certain RNAS units unofficially embellished their Camels in non-regulation markings prior to the formation of the RAF; as witnessed by this garish line-up of A Flight of 10(N) Squadron. Flight colours used for the zebra-stripes were Black/White (A); Red/White (B); and Blue/White (C Flight). Nearest Camel here, B6289, was one flown by the Canadian 'ace', W M Alexander. Pilots of the next two Camels were Lts F V Hall and D L Nelson.

"CAMEL" F.1. WHICH COLLIDED IN THE AIR AND LANDED SAFELY. – MAY 20/18

S.481.B.

CAMELS WERE RUGGED. D1851, 'X' of 70 Squadron which collided with D1796 of the same unit on May 20th, 1918 when formating. Its pilot, Lt W Gowen, and Lt S W Rochford in the other Camel both landed successfully without injuries. The individual name by the cockpit of 'X' was IKANOPIT . . .

Individual modifications in the light of combat experience were common on Camels. On this Camel of 73 Squadron (usually flown by succeeding commanding officers of the unit) the standard windscreen has been replaced by two separate screens along the left side of the guns. It also bears an insignia cartoon of a dog looking into a cupboard—a reference to one CO, Major T O'B Hubbard, MC and an old English nursery rhyme . . .

The 'loss' of these three units was soon compensated by the introduction of four more Camel squadrons. At Flez, 54 Squadron exchanged its Pups for Camels in mid-December, and was soon joined by three fresh squadrons from England. 73 Squadron at Lilbourne, Kent worked up to full strength with Camels and flew to France on January 9th, 1918, becoming based at Liettres; while 80 Squadron at Beverley, Yorkshire was fully operational by January and flew to Boisdinghem. The third newly-created unit was 4 (Australian Flying Corps) Squadron. Fully equipped with Camels in England, 4 AFC Squadron flew to Bruay airfield on December 18th. On January 6th, however, the Australians suffered a triple tragedy when three of their pilots collided during a routine formation flight and were all killed.** War flights commenced on January 13th, on which day a further loss was recorded when Lieutenant F.B. Wilmott in Camel B5602 had a complete engine failure over the lines and force-landed to become a prisoner of war. It was not until January 24th that 4 AFC Squadron opened its 'account', when Captain O'Hara Wood destroyed a DFW two-seater. Meanwhile 54 Squadron had begun its Camel operations and achieved the first unit victory on January 3rd (by Lieutenant H.G. Hackwill). With the return of 1 (N) Squadron to France on February 14th, 1918, by the beginning of March a total of 13 Camel squadrons were available for operations on the Western Front — Nos. 3, 43, 46, 54, 65, 73, 80 and 4 AFC with the RFC, and Nos. 3 (N), 8 (N), 9 (N), 10 (N) and 13 (N), working alongside their Army counterparts.

On March 3rd yet another Camel unit was added to front-line strength in France when 4 (N) Squadron flew from England to Bray Dunes, near Dunkirk, after two months' rest and refit. This squadron brought the total Camel strength on the Western Front to 336 machines with the operational squadrons, apart from an increasingly large reserve of new Camels and unserviceable aircraft at such aircraft depots as St Omer and Candas. The build-up of the Allied air services during the early months of 1918, though a logical progression of increased strength, was also a matter of urgency. With the defection of Russia from the war at the close of 1917, massive German reinforcements for the Western Front became possible at the turn of the year. With growing unrest internally, and the entry of America into the European conflict, Germany's need for a 'final decision' in the west had become vital, and the High Command prepared for a Spring offensive intended to force that 'decision.' German preparations were made almost openly, leaving little doubt in the Allies' minds as to its imminence. Preceded by a massive artillery bombardment, the German offensive commenced at 5 am on March 21st, 1918 along the whole frontage of the British Fifth and Third Armies from the Oise to the Scarpe, and the initial rapid advance towards Amiens overwhelmed the Allied infantry defenders.

Air support for the hard-pressed Allied infantry concentrated on deck-level strafing with bombs and bullets against the advancing German armies. Every aeroplane in the vicinity of the threatened front kept up a dawn to dusk series of sorties, returning to base only for more fuel and ammunition. Above the mists shrouding the land struggle the air was crowded with aircraft from the opposing air services. During air combat on the first day a total of 42 German aircraft was claimed by the RFC, while their own losses amounted to 11 missing, 46 wrecked, and a further eight destroyed or abandoned during hasty withdrawals from those first-line airfields coming within German artillery range. For the Camel pilots any air-to-air combat was incidental to their prime task — low-level strafing of German troops and guns. Hampered by bomb loads on the outward journey to the fighting zones, many Camels were relatively easy targets for marauding German fighters.

** F/n: Lts A.M. Anderson (B5217); R.H. Curtis (B4623); J.N. Cash (B2474).

Despite enforced amalgamation with the RFC in April 1918 to form the Royal Air Force, many former Naval units continued to apply colour markings to their machines. Here, Camels of 201 Squadron (formerly 1(N) Sqn) display various fin and wheel disc Flight colours, while nearest Camel, 'S' (F6022) also 'wore' black/white check livery on its tail surfaces. Scene at Bertangles, August 1918.

Hasty evacuation of prepared airfields in the face of the huge German land offensive of March 1918 caused most RFC units to be based in rough, uncultivated 'bases'. An example was 73 Squadron, whose Camels are seen here at a 'landing ground' near Humieres on April 6th, 1918, parked in the open. Overhead a Bristol F2b approaches for a landing.

IN DURANCE VILE. B5423, '6' of 54 Squadron in which Lt F M Ohrt, USAS was brought down in German lines on January 19th, 1918 and taken prisoner.

22

Prominent amongst the fighting Camel units was 4 (Australian Flying Corps) Squadron; some of whom's aircraft are seen here at Bruay on March 26th, 1918; each bearing the appropriate unit insigne of a white boomerang. Nearest Camel, B7406, 'W' was received by the unit on February 25th, and often flown by Lt H G Watson; while next in line is B7412, 'Y'.

PRISONER OF WAR. B5592, 'V' in which Lt A Couston of 4 (AFC) Sqn was brought down in enemy territory by Leutnant Matthaei of Jagdstaffel *46 on February 21st, 1918.*

Second Lieutenant D G 'Tommy' Lewis of 3 Squadron who became the 80th (last) claimed victim of the legendary Rittmeister Manfred von Richthofen on April 20th, 1918 in Camel B7393. He is seen here by his Camel of 78(HD) Squadron prior to service in France, B9309, RHODESIA— his private name to commemorate his country of birth, where he resides today (1977).

NAVAL FIGHTERS. FSL C A Narbeth standing by the nose of an F.1 Camel, DORIS, of 9(N) Sqn; a machine usually flown by Flight Commander Joseph S T Fall, DSC, July-August 1917.

YANKEE CAMELS. Line-up of the 148th Aero Squadron USAS at Petite Synthe, near Dunkirk, on August 6th, 1918. All carry the unit marking of a white triangle. The nearest machine, D9516, was lost on August 26th, 1918 and its pilot, Lt G V Siebold killed in action.

B7230, another 3(N) Squadron Camel, brought down behind German lines by anti-aircraft fire ('Archie) on March 10th, 1918. It's pilot, FSL K D Campbell, became a prisoner of war. Here the wings have been detached for ease of transport to a German aircraft depot.

26

During May 1918 the pace of air fighting was intensive, with heavy losses on both sides of the trenches; exemplified on the 10th when members of the *Richthofen Jagdgeschwader* accounted for ten Camels among their day's 'game bag.' It was also a month in which several veteran fighter pilots of the British and German air services made their last war sorties. On May 16th Captain S.T. Edwards in Camel B6398 of 209 Squadron shared with Lieutenants W.R. 'Wop' May and M.S. Taylor in forcing Leutnant Hübner of *Jagdstaffel* 4 to land his Fokker Triplane within British lines; while on May 30th another *Jasta* 4 pilot. Leutnant Viktor Rautter credited with 15 victories, was shot down by Captain A.W. Carter of 210 Squadron in Camel D3399. Three days before Carter's victory, however, the RAF lost one of its leading fighters when Captain D.J. Bell, MC of 3 Squadron was killed in combat, flying Camel C6730, the aircraft in which he had claimed eight of his total of 20 accredited victories. An indication of the tempo of the air fighting at that period is the week May 27th to June 2nd, during which, of the 149 German aircraft claimed by all RAF crews on the Western Front, 46 fell to Camel pilots.

In June 1918 the first American Camel unit was officially reformed for active service when the 17th Aero Squadron, USAS was declared 'operational' on June 20th. The unit's origin was in the USA on May 13th, 1917, and the squadron arrived in England on January 25th, 1918. Due to lack of aircraft and equipment its personnel were then dispersed among various RFC squadrons to gain experience. Eventually the ground crews, a few of the unit's original pilots, and many fresh pilots were assembled at Petite Synthe, near Dunkirk on June 20th and equipped with 110 hp Le Rhone-engined Camels. Lieutenant (later, Captain) S.B. Eckert was assigned as unit commander. Sam Eckert had seen active service already with 84 and 80 Squadrons RFC and the 9th Aero Squadron, USAS. By early July the 17th Aero was joined by a second American Camel unit, the 148th Aero Squadron, whose experience paralleled that of the 17th Aero. Arriving in England, the 148th Aero docked at Liverpool on March 6th, 1918 and was soon dispersed among British squadrons, including Nos 3, 54, 40, 70 and 208, just as the German Spring offensive was launched. On the last day of June these various 'detachments' were brought together at Cappelle airfield, Dunkirk, under the initial command of Lieutenant Morton Newhall, who had seen operational service with the British 3 and 84 Squadrons. Indeed, of the 21-pilot complement of the original 148th, eight were already combat-experienced, having been among the first English-trained American 'Warbirds' sent to Britain in 1917, and included Elliott White Springs, Bennett 'Bim' Oliver, Field Kindley, Erroll Zistel, Henry 'Hank' Clay, Harry Jenkinson, Lawrence Wyly and George Whiting.

Field Kindley, already credited with a victory over Leutnant Wilhelm Lehmann, commander of *Jagdstaffel* 5, on June 26th, 1918, whilst serving with 65 Squadron RAF; opened the American 'tally' on July 13th by shooting down an Albatros scout near Ypres. Seven days later Lieutenant R.D. Williams of the 17th Aero sent a Fokker D VII down out of control over Ostende to open his squadron's score-sheet. The same day saw the first loss for the 17th Aero when Lieutenant G. Glenn was shot down from 20,000 feet (sic!). On August 1st the 17th Aero registered its second official victory when Lieutenant R.M. Todd destroyed a Fokker Triplane near Provin, while other members of his patrol claimed three unconfirmed out of control victories. Two days later the unit claimed its third and fourth victims, but were soon in 'competition' with the 148th Aero when, on the same day, Springs and Kindley accounted for a pair of Fokker D VII's. With the start of the Allied ground offensive on August 8th, 1918 the 148th Aero was moved to the Amiens sector — at their own request — and became based at Allonsville; scoring six victories in their first week here. The squadron was then moved to Remaisnil, north-west of Doullens, and was attached to the 13th Wing, RAF.

As such, the Camels represented nearly 50 per cent of the 41 RAF and USAS fighter units on first-line strength. Of the other fighter squadrons, 12 were equipped with SE5A's, six with Bristol F2b's, and four with Sopwith Dolphins.

The varied and intensive operations undertaken by Camel pilots on the opening day of the offensive are perhaps typified by the exploits of several 201 Squadron men. Starting at 0530 hours, and carrying four 25lb Cooper bombs and full ammunition belts, the squadron's Camels took off at 30-minute intervals throughout the hours of daylight; bombing and machine-gunning enemy troops, transport, gun emplacements and supply vehicles at heights between 50 and 100 feet. Direct hits were recorded on three ammunition trains, six aircraft at Faucourt airfield, a dump at Cappy — resulting in a gigantic explosion — and the utter rout of hundreds of retreating German troops along roads behind the trenches. Lieutenant J.M. Mackay in particular had an eventful sortie shooting up a batch of German infantry. A trelliswork of intense ground fire brought his Camel down some 300 yards inside German-held territory. Unscathed, Mackay made a run for safety, met an advancing Allied tank and climbed aboard, then realised it was going 'the wrong way' so climbed off again and dodged through a hail of shell and small arms' fire to the relative safety of a forward British trench; eventually rejoining 201 Squadron later in the day. Elsewhere, Lieutenant Rollasson of 209 Squadron bombed parties of German infantry but his Camel was so badly damaged by the ground fire that he was forced to land near a British cavalry outpost. Remaining with the cavalry, Rollasson borrowed a rifle and continued his private war; eventually arriving back at his airfield astride a borrowed horse . . .'

High above the battle air fighting reached a new peak of intensity and in the period August 5th to 11th the RAF claimed 276 German aircraft and balloons as destroyed or brought down, for the overall loss of 93 RAF machines — the highest claims figures of any comparative period of the entire war. Again, several of the losses on both sides were of veteran pilots. On August 12th Captain R.M. Foster in Camel C61 of 209 Squadron forced down Offizierstvtr Blumenthal in a Fokker D VII; while on the 13th 201 Squadron's commander, Major C.D. Booker, DSO, DSC, flying Camel D9642, attempted to rescue another Camel pilot from the attentions of several Fokkers, only to be seriously wounded. Returning to the British lines, Booker crashed and soon died of his multiple injuries.

By September 1918 the Allied advance had begun to penetrate deep into German-held territory, and the air services now concentrated on pursuing the retreating German armies. Work on the Camel squadrons evolved into two major facets — continual harassment of German airfields and fierce, massed dogfights with the far from defunct German Imperial Air Service. It was a period when opposing formations of (mainly) fighters met and fought in sprawling dogfights, involving 60,80 or even 100 aircraft, spread at all levels across the sky. The heroic days of the lone fighter were over — safety and success lay in numbers and the co-ordinated effort of whole squadrons working as fighting teams. Even so, the ferocity with which the German *jagdstaffeln* fought during the closing weeks of the war claimed high losses among the Camel units. On September 4th, 70 Squadron took off in strength at 0720 hours on an Offensive Patrol (OP) over Escaillon and became involved with several enemy formations; losing eight Camels in a mere 20 minutes' fighting. On the 28th a morning patrol from 65 Squadron lost six Camels over the Ostende region.

A combined raid on September 26th saw the Camels of 203 Squadron join forces with eleven SE5A's of 40 Squadron to attack Lieu St Amand airfield, with an aerial top cover of Bristol F2b's of 22 Squadron. The SE's attacked the aerodrome first, bombing a large hangar and several wooden huts, then 203 swept across the field low and left three other hangars in flames and a fourth totally wrecked. Spotting one German aircraft valiantly attempting to take off, Ray Collishaw quickly destroyed it, and on the return journey the Camel pilots accounted for four more German aircraft encountered. The pattern of this raid was repeated on October 5th when three Australian Camel pilots of 4 AFC Squadron destroyed an observation balloon, bombed a train in Avelin station, strafed Avelin airfield, wrecked a gun battery, attacked several horse-drawn transports, and rounded out their foray of 70-minutes' action by blowing up two trucks of a goods train.

Lt Field Kindley, commander of 'A' Flight, 148th Aero Squadron, USAS with his pet dog, 'Fokker'.

AUSSIES. Members of 4(AFC) Squadron at Clairmarais, May 1918. L-R: Lts J H Weingarth; G G Smallwood; R C Nelson; R C Nelson; W S Martin; and A T Heller.

On August 13th, meanwhile, the 17th Aero joined with 210 and 213 Squadrons, RAF in a combined attack on the German airfield at Varssenaere, south-west of Bruges. Taking turns to bomb and then protect the other units, all three Camel units created havoc on the objective; destroying 14 German aircraft, killing 30 pilots and 120 mechanics, and demolishing numerous hangars and other structures. All Camels returned safely, albeit scarred and tattered with the effect of an intensive ground fire at the target. On August 18th the 17th Aero moved base to Auxi-le-Chateau in the Amiens area and soon ran into trouble against several 'crack' German *jagdstaffeln;* losing ten pilots, killed, wounded or missing during their first week, including two of the three Flight commanders. An even heavier blow came on August 26th, when the squadron lost six of an eleven-aircraft patrol to elements of *Jagdstaffel Boelcke* and other top quality opponents. Though five victories were claimed from this fight, the squadron was temporarily withdrawn from action for a few days while fresh aircraft and pilots were ferried in. One of the replacement Flight commanders to arrive was George Vaughn, already an 'ace' from his service with 84 Squadron, RAF.

The 148th Aero fared better during this period, claiming 30 victories during the month August 18th to September 20th, for a loss of six pilots; four of these in one fight on September 2nd. As the Allied offensive surged eastwards, both American Camel units were moved forward in support; the 148th transferring to Baizieux, near Albert on September 20th, and the 17th going to Soncamp, near Doullens on the same date. On September 22nd the 17th Aero reopened their 'account' in fine style when George Vaughn led his patrol down on 15 Fokker D VII's and claimed five Fokkers for the loss of two Camel pilots. Two days later the unit claimed four more Fokkers. Not to be outshone, the 148th scored a resounding success on September 24th when 15 Camels tackled 20 Fokker D VII's and shot down seven for only one 'loss'. The latter 'loss' was Errol Zistel who became unconscious during the fight and regained consciousness in a casualty clearing station near Bapaume four days later. . .' Only two days later the Camels of the 148th Aero claimed four Fokker D VII's from a vicious dogfight over Bourlon Wood.

Particularly noteworthy 'solo' sortie was that undertaken by Field Kindley on September 27th. Loaded with Cooper bombs, he set out to strafe German transport; then turned his attention to a German observation balloon. Puncturing the *drachen* with some 200 rounds, Kindley was engaged by a Halberstadt two-seater which he destroyed in flames for his 11th confirmed victory. Using up his remaining ammunition on retreating German infantry, he next spotted two Fokker D VII's attacking a lone Camel and, despite his empty ammunition belts, dived in to 'frighten them off. . .' His bluff succeeded and he returned to Baizieux. His work that morning brought him an Oak Leaf Cluster to his Distinguished Service Cross and a British Distinguished Flying Cross. In the same morning Elliott White Springs scored his 12th (and last) official victory, sharing the destruction of a Halberstadt with Henry Clay.

During October the 148th was credited with ten German aircraft brought down, and seven of these came on October 28th when all three Flights set an aerial trap for seven Fokker D VII's and then destroyed them in a series of furious dogfights; Field Kindley registering his 12th victory in the melee. On November 1st both the 17th and 148th Aero Squadrons were transferred to Tou airfield, some 150 miles from Paris, where both units were assigned to the 4th Pursuit Group, USAS and re-equipped with Spad scouts. Before re-equipment was complete, however, the war had ended Several other Camel squadrons were formed by the USAS during the closing weeks of the war, but only one, the 185th Aero Squadron, a night-fighter unit, saw any active service before the Armistice.

TAXI RANK. Camels of the 148th Aero Squadron USAS about to take off from Petite Synthe, August 6th, 1918.

WAR-BIRD. Captain Elliott White Springs of 148th Aero Squadron USAS after a ground accident to his Camel. Springs previously saw combat with 85 Squadron RAF (SE5A's) before being transferred to the 148th; and is known internationally for his editorship of the classic WW1 aviation diary, WAR BIRDS.

Camel flown by Captain Henry R Clay, Jr, commander of the 41st Aero Squadron, USAS in late 1918; bearing the unit marking of a camel (desert variety) in a 'V'. 'Hank' Clay saw active combat previously with another Camel unit, 43 Squadron RAF.

The Allied land offensive which commenced on August 8th, 1918 was preceded by a build-up of all air services. The increase in strength was parallelled by the more intensive tempo of aerial activity, particularly in pure combat. Throughout June and July the more successful Camel pilots had added a large number of victories to individual scores. The Canadian commander of 203 Squadron, Ray Collishaw, returned from leave in early June and immediately scored victories; while on July 1st Captain John Gilmour of 65 Squadron brought down four opponents in one patrol. The Australian top-scorer Arthur Cobby of 4 AFC Squadron claimed a triple victory on June 28th. Against such successes must be set the loss of such veteran fighters as Major R.H. Freeman, MC, commander of 73 Squadron, who failed to return from a patrol on July 21st in Camel D1918. In strict terms of technical superiority, by July 1918 the Camel had virtually reached its peak and was beginning to meet new German fighters, like the Fokker D VII, which could out-run and out-climb it. Nevertheless, in experienced hands the Camel's superlative manoeuvrability could — and did — prove lethal to any opponent, given a fight on its own terms. By the end of July 1918 a new vogue in Camel operations began to be implemented whereby a whole squadron or combination of several units undertook low-level strafing missions against German airfields, attempting to nullify German air strength before the imminent August 'push'. Two very experienced Camel pilots of 203 Squadron gave a splendid example of what might be achieved in this mode of attack when, on July 22nd, Major Ray Collishaw and Captain L.H. 'Tich' Rochford set out at dawn to raid Dorignies airfield. Attacking first, Rochford fired all his ammunition from 200 feet into hangars and huts, then released three 25lb bombs on personnel accommodation and a fourth Cooper bomb into a hangar which immediately erupted in flames. Collishaw strafed three aircraft being hastily removed from another hangar, and then bombed some adjacent huts. He next attacked a German aircraft as it attempted to land and destroyed it in flames. Two hours later Collishaw returned to check damage and was jumped by three Albatros Scouts; one of which he promptly destroyed.

On August 8th, 1918 the massive Allied ground offensive swung into action. On that day a total of 19 Camel squadrons were available for operations, located as under:

Squadron	Commander	Base
3	Major R St Clair McClintock	Valheureux
43	Major C C Miles	Fienvillers
46	Major A H O'Hara Wood	Serny
54	Major R S Maxwell	Fienvillers
65	Major H V C de Crespigny	Bertangles
70	Major E L Foot	Esquerdes
73	Major M Le Blanc-Smith	Bellevue
80	Major V D Bell	Vignacourt
151**	Major C J Q Brand	Fontaine-sur-Maye
201	Major C D Booker	Poulainville
203	Major R Collishaw	Le Hameau
204	Major E W Norton	Teteghem
208	Major C Draper	Tramecourt
209	Major J O Andrews	Poulainville
210	Major B C Bell	Eringham
213	Major R Graham	Bergues
4 AFC	Major W A McClaughry	Reclinghem
17th Aero	Lt E B Eckert, USAS	Petite Synthe
148th Aero	Lt M L Newhall, USAS	Cappelle

**For night fighting duties only

When Escadrille 9 of the Belgian Air Service exchanged its Camels for Hanriot HD 1's, the Camels were taken over by Escadrille 11; marked as here. Pilot is Van de Voordt.

Camel F1360, one of several hundreds transferred and/or bought by the American Air Services.

At least 50 Camels were transferred to the Belgian air service in 1918. One of Belgium's outstanding pilots was Jan Oesliegers, seen here by an Escadrille 9 Camel, SK7, bearing the unit marking of a thistle. On top of the fuselage is the motto NEMO ME IMPUNE LACESSIT. Note also the green/white markings on engine cowling and tail surfaces.

READY TO GO. Lieutenant F T S Sehl, a Canadian, at the controls. Note pilot's windscreen located well forward of cockpit.

33

As such, the Camels represented nearly 50 per cent of the 41 RAF and USAS fighter units on first-line strength. Of the other fighter squadrons, 12 were equipped with SE5A's, six with Bristol F2b's, and four with Sopwith Dolphins.

The varied and intensive operations undertaken by Camel pilots on the opening day of the offensive are perhaps typified by the exploits of several 201 Squadron men. Starting at 0530 hours, and carrying four 25lb Cooper bombs and full ammunition belts, the squadron's Camels took off at 30-minute intervals throughout the hours of daylight; bombing and machine-gunning enemy troops, transport, gun emplacements and supply vehicles at heights between 50 and 100 feet. Direct hits were recorded on three ammunition trains, six aircraft at Faucourt airfield, a dump at Cappy — resulting in a gigantic explosion — and the utter rout of hundreds of retreating German troops along roads behind the trenches. Lieutenant J.M. Mackay in particular had an eventful sortie shooting up a batch of German infantry. A trelliswork of intense ground fire brought his Camel down some 200 yards inside German-held territory. Unscathed, Mackay made a run for safety, met an advancing Allied tank and climbed aboard, then realised it was going 'the wrong way' so climbed off again and dodged through a hail of shell and small arms' fire to the relative safety of a forward British trench; eventually rejoining 201 Squadron later in the day. Elsewhere, Lieutenant Rollasson of 209 Squadron bombed parties of German infantry but his Camel was so badly damaged by the ground fire that he was forced to land near a British cavalry outpost. Remaining with the cavalry, Rollasson borrowed a rifle and continued his private war; eventually arriving back at his airfield astride a borrowed horse . . .'

High above the battle air fighting reached a new peak of intensity and in the period August 5th to 11th the RAF claimed 276 German aircraft and balloons as destroyed or brought down, for the overall loss of 93 RAF machines — the highest claims figures of any comparative period of the entire war. Again, several of the losses on both sides were of veteran pilots. On August 12th Captain R.M. Foster in Camel C61 of 209 Squadron forced down Offizierstvtr Blumenthal in a Fokker D VII; while on the 13th 201 Squadron's commander, Major C.D. Booker, DSO, DSC, flying Camel D9642, attempted to rescue another Camel pilot from the attentions of several Fokkers, only to be seriously wounded. Returning to the British lines, Booker crashed and soon died of his multiple injuries.

By September 1918 the Allied advance had begun to penetrate deep into German-held territory, and the air services now concentrated on pursuing the retreating German armies. Work on the Camel squadrons evolved into two major facets — continual harassment of German airfields and fierce, massed dogfights with the far from defunct German Imperial Air Service. It was a period when opposing formations of (mainly) fighters met and fought in sprawling dogfights, involving 60,80 or even 100 aircraft, spread at all levels across the sky. The heroic days of the lone fighter were over — safety and success lay in numbers and the co-ordinated effort of whole squadrons working as fighting teams. Even so, the ferocity with which the German *jagdstaffeln* fought during the closing weeks of the war claimed high losses among the Camel units. On September 4th, 70 Squadron took off in strength at 0720 hours on an Offensive Patrol (OP) over Escaillon and became involved with several enemy formations; losing eight Camels in a mere 20 minutes' fighting. On the 28th a morning patrol from 65 Squadron lost six Camels over the Ostende region.

A combined raid on September 26th saw the Camels of 203 Squadron join forces with eleven SE5A's of 40 Squadron to attack Lieu St Amand airfield, with an aerial top cover of Bristol F2b's of 22 Squadron. The SE's attacked the aerodrome first, bombing a large hangar and several wooden huts, then 203 swept across the field low and left three other hangars in flames and a fourth totally wrecked. Spotting one German aircraft valiantly attempting to take off, Ray Collishaw quickly destroyed it, and on the return journey the Camel pilots accounted for four more German aircraft encountered. The pattern of this raid was repeated on October 5th when three Australian Camel pilots of 4 AFC Squadron destroyed an observation balloon, bombed a train in Avelin station, strafed Avelin airfield, wrecked a gun battery, attacked several horse-drawn transports, and rounded out their foray of 70-minutes' action by blowing up two trucks of a goods train.

CANUCKS. Personnel of 203 Squadron, Izel le Hameau, July 10th, 1918—nearly all of whom were Canadian-born. Rear, L-R: F T S Sehl; Y E S Kirkpatrick; F C Black; R Stone; H Nelson; E F Adams; C H Lick; J D Breakey; A E Rudge. Centre; L D Bawlf; A T Whealey; H F Beamish; Maj R Collishaw (OC); L H Rochford; E T Hayne; D A Haig (Armament officer). Front: W Sidebottom; W A W Carter; J E L Hunter; P W Bingham (Recording Officer); W Towell (Equipment); N C Dixie; F J S Britnell.

203 Squadron's Camels at Izel le Hameau on July 10th, 1918; the occasion of a review by HM King George V. Nearest machine is D3417, in which the squadron commander, Major Ray Collishaw, claimed at least 17 victories. It was also flown by his successor, Major T F Hazell, DSO, MC, DFC, and Captain L Rochford, DSC, DFC. Next Camel in line is B3809, named 'NIBS'.

In the air the reign of destruction continued apace. On October 9th Captain S.T. Liversedge led a patrol of 70 Squadron's Camels and destroyed one of a pair of LVG two-seaters over Courtrai but was then attacked by eight Fokker D VIII's. Within minutes five of the Fokkers were destroyed. A mass dogfight involving more than 50 fighters took place on October 27th, when sixteen Camels of 204 Squadron engaged nearly 40 Fokkers over St Denis Westrem; claiming four Fokkers destroyed; By mid-October the German armies were evacuating Belgium and on the 17th many reconnaissance sorties were flown to ascertain the latest locations of German troops. One Camel pilot landed on Ghistelles aerodrome, only to find the former German base deserted. Another Camel, from 210 Squadron, landed in Ostende market square, where he was attacked by nearly a dozen German soldiers about to evacuate the city. By the end of the month RAF squadrons were in possession of all former German airfields in Belgium.

During the first ten days of November 1918 air activity continued at a high pitch over the crumbling Western Front, and indeed remained intensive until the eventual cease-fire. The German *jagdstaffeln,* desperately short of fuel, supplies and replacements, were still capable of bitter opposition but their gallant efforts were in vain — the end for Germany was now inevitable. On the morning of November 11th orders were issued to every unit of the RAF that hostilities were to cease at 1100 hours that day, and no aircraft was to fly beyond the most forward position reached by Allied infantry at that hour. It is perhaps significant of the keyed-up states of mind of many Camel (and other) pilots of the RAF that just before the eleventh hour few aircraft were on the ground. And when the last fighters returned from their 'last look at the war. . .' many bomb racks and ammunition belts were suspiciously empty. . .

For the first few months of the 'peace' the Camel units were employed as elements of the Allied occupation forces in Germany, but rapid demobilisation of personnel quickly reduced the squadrons to mere skeletons of their former strengths. By March 1919 a majority of squadrons were merely of cadre strength and were returned to England to '. . . await further disposition' (sic). The post-Armistice disinterest in military strength or indeed any form of war material led to a drastic reduction of RAF units.

Of the eighteen Camel squadrons existing in November 1918, none survived beyond January 1920. The disbandment dates for the Camel squadrons indicate how rapidly the Royal Air Force — the world's largest, and first independent air service — was dissipated.

Squadron	Disbanded	Location
3	October 27th, 1919	Dover
43	December 31st, 1919	Spittlegate
45	December 31st, 1919	Eastleigh
46	December 31st, 1919	Rendcombe
54	October 25th, 1919	Yatesbury
65	October 25th, 1919	Yatesbury
70	January 22nd, 1920	Spittlegate
73	July 2nd, 1919	Yatesbury
80	Re-equipped with Sopwith Snipes, December 1918	
201	December 31st, 1919	Lake Down
203	January 21st, 1920	Scopwick
204	December 31st, 1919	Waddington
208	November 7th, 1919	Netheravon
209	June 24th, 1919	Scopwick
210	June 24th, 1919	Scopwick
213	December 31st, 1919	Scopwick

HOW THEY CAME BACK. F.1 Camel, F1941, 'P' of 73 Squadron (Lt R N Chandler) which returned safely to base after an 18-pounder shell had ripped through the upper fuselage decking. This machine also saw service with 4(AFC) Squadron. It was originally a presentation machine, titled 'New South Wales No.9, The Tweed, Presented by residents and district of Tweed River'.

FIGHTER-BOMBER.   Captain A T 'Art' Whealey, DSC, a Canadian of 203 Squadron, watches air mechanics loading his F.1 Camel's under-fuselage racks with four 25lb Cooper bombs. July 1918 at Izel le Hameau aerodrome, France.

IN ITALIAN SKIES

On October 24th, 1917 an Austro-German offensive, directed by the German general staff, was launched against the Italian armies in a 'final' bid to shatter Italian opposition. The spearhead of this offensive centred on Caporetto, where Italian defences quickly crumpled and left a wide gap for Austrian troops to exploit. By November 10th Austrian advance formations had reached westwards to the Piave river but due to lack of adequate reserves and material were unable to pursue their success. Acutely aware of the possibility of an Italian defeat, the French and British governments agreed on October 26th to supply divisions from the Western Front to bolster the Italian armies; and for added air co-operation, 28 Squadron (Camels) and 34 Squadron (RE8's) were withdrawn from France, grouped to form a new RFC Wing, the 51st, and despatched by train to Italy, commencing this move on November 7th. A further agreement for more aerial support resulted in two more Camel units, 45 and 66 Squadrons, being ordered from France to the Italian front. 66 Squadron began its transfer on November 17th; while 45 Squadron set off in two trains on December 11th and 12th. This latest increase in air strength necessitated the formation of VII Brigade to administer all RFC air units in Italy.

Nos 28 and 34 Squadrons reached Milan on November 12th and 14th respectively, and by a great effort on the part of 28's ground crews the squadron's Camels were assembled and declared fit for operations within 48 hours of arrival On November 22nd the Camels moved to Verona, and six days later moved again, to Grossa airfield. Meantime 66 Squadron arrived and occupied Verona initially, before joining 28 Squadron at Grossa on December 4th. The remaining Camel unit, 45 arrived safely and on Christmas Day moved to Istrana aerodrome. Almost immediately all three Camel units became busily engaged in a daily routine of operations. The normal pattern was for three Camels at a time to maintain general offensive patrols at around 10,000 feet from dawn to dusk over the Piave and Asiago fronts; while as many as six Camels were usually provided as escort for the RE8 reconnaissance sorties undertaken by 34 Squadron. Combat between the Camels and their Austro-Hungarian counterparts were infrequent at first, though as the new year 1918 commenced air fighting gradually increased in intensity. Until the arrival of the RFC Austrian fighter pilots had found their task of protecting their reconnaissance aircraft a relatively easy one; with the 'stiffening' of several German *jagdstaffeln* provided for the original October 1917 offensive, including *Jagdstaffeln* 1, 31 and 39, had virtually gained aerial supremacy over the whole Italian front. However, with the Austrian offensive halted along the Piave and the imminent German offensive in France, the German fighter units were quickly withdrawn and sent back to the Western Front. *Jagdstaffel* 1 left its base at San Fior on March 13th, 1918, while pilots from *Jastas* 31 and 39 were gradually transferred to France during the same period. By the end of March most (if not all) German fighter pilots had left Italy for France.

On March 30th, 1918 three Camels of 66 Squadron left their airfield at San Pietro-in-Gu for an offensive patrol. The pilots were Captain P. Carpenter (Camel, B7387), Lieutenant H.R. Eycott-Martin (B7283) and Lieutenant Alan Jerrard (B5648, 'E'). It was a routine patrol, a general hunt for enemy aircraft, but before the day was out Alan Jerrard was to become the only Camel pilot ever to be eventually awarded a Victoria Cross. Just before noon the Camel trio were in the vicinity of Ghirano airfield behind Austrian lines and saw below them four Oeffag-built Albatros D III's obviously about to land. Led by Jerrard the Camels at once dived hard out of the sun. Below them the D III's were about to complete an escort mission, having already seen their 'charge', a two-seater of *Fliegerkompagnie* (Flik) 32, safely to its own base. The quartet of Albatri were from Flik 51J and led by the noted Austrian 'ace' Oberleutnant Benno Fiala von Fernbrugg. Jerrard was the first Camel pilot to engage, tackling one Albatros and becoming immediately engrossed in a series of tail-chasing turns. A second Camel attacked von Fernbrugg from above, but the veteran Austrian pulled the nose of his Albatros up and liberally sprayed his assailant from below. Fernbrugg's wing man, Stefan Fejes, then engaged this second Camel, forcing it to turn southwards towards the Piave river.

Line-up of 28 Squadron in Italy at the close of 1917. Nearest three machines are, respectively, B5169 ('3'); B6363 ('C2'); and W G Barker's famous B6313 ('1'). The white square was the unit marking for all squadron Camels. B6363 had previously served with 13(N) Squadron, and was later 'K' in 28 Squadron; having at least six victories claimed by its various pilots.

Camels of 45 Squadron on Istrana airfield, Italy, January 1918.

Left: Lieutenant Alan Jerrard, VC, the only Camel pilot to be awarded a Victoria Cross.

Above: Jerrard's Camel, B5648, 'E' of 66 Squadron, after his combat of March 30th, 1918.

Below: Alan Jerrard, dazed and in shock, sitting beside the wreckage of his Camel, B5648, 'E' on March 30th, 1918. On the ground, at his left, is his leather face mask, helmet and goggles.

Resuming his former course to the south-west, Fernbrugg found himself heading directly at Jerrard's Camel which was approaching him head-on. As the two fighters rapidly closed the range von Fernbrugg opened fire, splashing about 100 rounds in one long burst into the blunt nose of his opponent's machine. Jerrard pushed the nose of his Camel downwards and headed for the Italian lines. Turning 180-degrees swiftly, von Fernbrugg tucked in behind the fleeing Camel and loosed off another 100 rounds; being joined in his attack by another Albatros, piloted by Stabsfeldwebel Boensch. Jerrard's engine suddenly stopped and Boensch withdrew from the pursuit, leaving his commander von Fernbrugg to 'finish him off.' Forced to land, Jerrard picked a meadow surrounded by willow trees, two miles due south of Mansue airfield at Gorgo al Montico. As he flattened out to land Jerrard's Camel hit a tree, tearing away its port wings, bounced viciously and hit the ground, breaking off its tail assembly; then slithered across the meadow tipped up on its nose until it halted. Luckily for Jerrard there was no fire, and he was extricated from the wreckage suffering from multiple bruising and rather severe shock but otherwise unharmed. His conqueror landed immediately at Ghirano airfield, some four kilometres away, and rushed by car to the scene. The meeting between 'victor' and 'vanquished' was cordial and von Fernbrugg then took Jerrard by car to the Austrian Army headquarters at Oderzo.

Examination of Jerrard's Camel wreck revealed a total of 163 bullet strikes, 27 of them in the main fuel tank and 16 in the engine. The fuel-loss from the ruptured petrol tank while still in the air had probably saved Jerrard from a fiery end. At his interrogation Jerrard merely claimed one victory from the fight, and Austrian records indicate that the only casualties on the Austrian side from this combat were Fejes with a light foot wound, and a second Albatros which was forced to land at Ghirano with its engine coolant pipe broken by a stray bullet. Alan Jerrard, the 14th confirmed victory of Benno Fiala von Fernbrugg, was later awarded a Victoria Cross; its citation appearing in the London Gazette dated May 1st 1918 and closely based on the post-combat reports of Jerrard's fellow pilots, Carpenter and Eycott-Martin (or so it would appear). The citation description of Jerrard's last combat differs from the known facts of the combat; though it should be emphasised that Jerrard himself had no part in the various stages of recommendation which led to his supreme award. Remaining in the RAF after the war, Alan Jerrard eventually retired from the Service as a Flight Lieutenant in August 1933, and died on May 14th, 1968.

Throughout April 1918 weather conditions over the whole Italian front were mostly stormy, permitting relatively little air activity, but in May the weather improved considerably and air operations on both sides intensified. The German Spring offensive in France had immediate repercussions on the British air formation in Italy at this time. A large part of the 51st Brigade was hastily returned to France during March 1918, leaving only the 14th Wing, comprised of 28,45 and 66 Squadrons (Camels), 34 Squadron (RE8's), 9th Balloon Company, and the 7th Aircraft Park. A Flight of Bristol F2b two-seater fighters arrived from England and was temporarily attached to 28 Squadron, but soon moved to join 34 Squadron. Known initially as Z Flight, these Bristols later became the nucleus of a full squadron, No. 139, RAF. The reduction in pure numerical strength was to a great degree offset by the constant activity of the three Camel units, and during the first three months of 1918 these firmly established Allied air supremacy over the Italian front. Leading Camel pilots such as George Barker, John Mitchell, Clifford McEwen, 'Spike' Howell and Matthew Frew — merely to name a few — were soon scoring victories almost daily.

An example of the pace of fighting was a patrol of 45 Squadron's Camels on January 15th, when Captain M.B. Frew led his men over the lines, seeking Austrian aircraft. Spotting an enemy two-seater escorted by four scouts, Frew led his patrol eastwards of these and then dived from 12,000 feet onto the two-seater. His first four rounds were sufficient to send the two-seater spinning to earth in flames. With one Vickers gun jammed, Frew next tackled two of the Austrian fighters and eventually shot down both. He then attacked another Austrian engaged with one Camel and sent it down wildly out of control. The Camels re-formed behind Frew who led them towards the lines, but ran into a furious barrage of anti-aircraft fire. Frew's Camel received a direct hit, slicing away one wheel and causing extensive damage to the engine and upper wing. Frew switched off his engine and flat-glided towards the Piave river, running helplessly into yet more groundfire. By the time he reached the river he was dangerously low and only by momentarily switching on his engine did he manage to cross into Italian-held territory, finally crash-landing near Saletto. The crash injured Frew's neck, resulting in his return to England shortly afterwards; but this combat had brought his victory tally to 24, and he managed to add three more victories before leaving Italy — thus establishing himself as 45 Squadron's highest-scoring pilot. On January 26th another 45 Squadron pilot, T.F. Williams, scored a particularly unusual victory. Returning from one combat, he noticed a lone Austrian scout flying towards the Allied kite balloon lines. Williams lined himself up for an attack but found that his Aldis gun sight was fogged. Having no ring and bead sight fixed to his guns, he decided to 'sight' by watching his tracer ammunition and accordingly fired three of four rounds from one gun. The Austrian promptly turned 180-degrees, whereupon William lightly tripped his other and fired four more rounds. The result was immediate and the Austrian scout '. . . crumpled like a deck of cards. . .'; the wreckage plunging through the roof of a house some 3,000 feet below.

Air fighting was not the only duty for the Camel squadrons. On February 19th an 'experimental' raid was mounted by 12 Camels, six from each of 28 and 66 Squadrons, with the objective of attacking an Austrian airship complex at Casarsa, reported as being in use as an aircraft park. Each Camel was loaded with four 25lb Cooper bombs, and the two formations flew to their target at less than 100 feet to avoid detection by the ground gunners. Over Casarsa the Camels rose to 300 feet and attacked; their bombs making at least eleven direct hits on two large airship sheds, while a nearby railway truck erupted in an explosion of flames. The success of this mode of surprise raid led to further similar low-level bombing strafes and the technique for such attacks became well used. Approach to target was always at virtually ground level, with the Camels' wheels almost brushing the terrain. The leading Camel was responsible for clearing a path through any alert ground defences and its pilot usually flew literally with his thumbs resting lightly poised over his gun trigger levers. Whilst he kept the ground defences 'head-down' the bombing Camels went into the target by one route and invariably left by a second route to confuse any opposition.

Although the bad weather conditions of April 1918 curtailed most Allied air operations, occasional combats continued to exemplify the Camels' supremacy. On April 17th, for example, four Camels from 28 Squadron led by Captain John Mitchell were 'jumped' from above by five scarlet-hued Albatros D III's. In only five minutes of fierce fighting all four Camel pilots claimed a victim apiece, with the sole surviving D III escaping hurriedly to the east and safety. Reconnaissance RE8's and Bristol F2b's now began bringing back partial evidence of a possible Austrian ground assault being imminent in the Val Sugana sector. To counter this threat an Allied offensive was planned in mid-May to be launched in the Asiago region. Then, as yet more evidence became available of the Austrian build-up, it was decided to postpone the Anglo-Italian 'push' and all Allied efforts were concentrated on dissipating the Austrian coming offensive. On the morning of May 30th a total of 35 Camels were despatched to bomb and strafe enemy troop accommodation in the Val d'Assa area. Twelve 'bomber' and three 'escort' Camels were supplied by 28 Squadron, with Ghertele as their specific objective; whilst the remaining 20 Camels came from 45 and 66 Squadrons. The operational directive indicated that all bombing had to be carried out from below 500 feet, with 100 yard intervals between aircraft on the run-in. Over the targets the Camels released a ton of high explosive and fired more than 9,000 rounds; scoring at least 28 direct hits with their Cooper bombs.

YOU BEND 'EM, WE MEND 'EM—the motto of the long-toiling ground crews. Camel B3840, 'F' of 66 Squadron being retrieved from a minor ground accident. This particular Camel had an unfortunate career. Issued initially to 70 Squadron, it was crashed and returned to depot on August 16th, 1917; was re-issued to 66 Squadron; and finally crashed again on May 2nd, 1918, killing its pilot Lt W H Robinson.

Third of the trio of Camel units in Italy was 66 Squadron; one of its Camels being D8101, 'P', here, flown by Lt Gerald Birks. Unit marking was a horizontal white line abaft the cockade, and a vertical white bar in front. In this view the engine is removed for routine servicing.

B6345, 'F' of 28 Squadron, in which
Captain C J Thompson was shot down
and made prisoner of war on April
23rd, 1918, Italy.

B6238, 'C' of 45 Squadron, a Camel
flown variously by Lt R J Brownell,
MC, MM, and Captain Matthew Frew,
DSO, MC.

Captain M B Frew, DSO, MC (left) of
45 Squadron, with his Camel, B6372,
at Istrana, December 1917. This
machine had seen previous service
with 8(N) Squadron in France.

Despite the 'loss' of their 'star turn' George Barker in April, when he was transferred to 66 Squadron, 28 Squadron's pilots continued to add to the unit's mounting tally. In May 1918 a total of 25 victories was claimed, for the loss of one pilot (a prisoner of war); whilst June brought further claims for 22 victories to be set against the losses of five pilots. Prominent among the unit's pilots at this time were the Canadian Clifford McEwen, T.F. Williams, Stan Stanger, John Mitchell, H.B. Hudson and P. Wilson.

The long-expected Austrian offensive finally erupted along the whole front on the morning of June 15th, 1918 stretching from the sea to positions east of Astico, and preceded by a violent if relatively brief artillery bombardment. Initially Austrian infantry penetrated the Piave front in several places, and occupied commanding positions in the hilly region of Montello; thereby posing a threat to Allied positions on the Asiago plateau. In spite of atrocious weather conditions the Camels of 28, 45 and 66 Squadrons were called upon to help obviate the massive onslaught. The biggest threat was in the Italian-held sections of the front, where dozens of pontoon bridges were being erected across the Piave, permitting huge numbers of reserve and 'back-up' Austrian troops easy crossings to the fighting zones. Loaded fully with Cooper bombs and ammunition the Camels of 28 Squadron were in action from 0325 hours until darkness fell that evening. A brief extract from the personal diary of one 28 Squadron pilot, Tom Williams, gives an inkling of the turmoil of these operations; '. . . Instead of making any move to retreat++, we concentrated on splashing massed Austrians with our Cooper bombs and gunning them at such close range that we could see the expressions on the men's faces. We kept this up until dark, when my Flight ('A') had a toll of one dead**, one missing, and one wounded.'

In the evening Captain Stan Stanger was one of nine 28 Squadron pilots detailed to bomb Austrian infantry crossing the Piave by five pontoon bridges. Stanger obtained four direct hits on the head of one bridge and then exhausted his ammunition in strafing troops and bridge repair gangs. His attack was later estimated to have routed some 3,000 troops; with a comparison of after-patrol reports indicating casualties of at least 500. Elsewhere the air and ground battles raged equally fiercely. Just after 1600 hours a total of 33 Camels were supplementing Italian aircraft in wreaking havoc amongst the first-line enemy soldiers. Captain George Barker, now a Flight commander with 66 Squadron, recorded; 'The Montello, owing to its height, dominated the Venetian plain and under its cover they (the Austrian infantry) had thrown two pontoon bridges across the river. The leader (of the Camels) selected a bridge farthest up-stream and individual bombing commenced from about 50 feet. This bridge was quickly broken in two places and the pontoons, caught by the fast current, were immediately dashed against the lower bridge, carrying it away also. When this attack commenced the bridges were crowded with troops which were attacked with machine gun fire. Many were seen to be in the water. This done, troops on small islands and in row boats were machine-gunned. . .'

Air-to-air activity was equally intensive, and 28 Squadron's Camels claimed five victories throughout the day; but the main effort remained the necessity to stem the ground attack. A further extract from Captain T.F. Williams' diary continues the story; 'The next morning (June 16th) my mission was to destroy a bridge on the lower Piave where the enemy had advanced for some 14 miles over. It was raining and fog was at tree-top height but the plains were level. I had five pilots. As we neared the pontoon bridge they fell into line astern, letting all four bombs go at the one pass. I led and kept machine-gunning the area . . . until the operation was concluded. We each went back to the airfield separately, avoiding the area we had alerted going over, except for Lieutenant S.W. Ellison (Camel B5204) who was caught when he was nearly over occupied ground. He died in Mogliano hospital within a few hours.' Throughout the day (16th) approximately two tons of 25lb

++ F/n: 28 Squadron had received orders to be prepared for evacuation at 15 minutes' notice.

** F/n: Lt J.G. Russell, in Camel B7351, crashed and later died in hospital.

Above: CAMEL 'ACES'. Captains N C Jones (left) and the top-scoring Canadian-pilot, Clifford M McEwen, both of 28 Squadron. Seen here at Yatesbury, England shortly after the unit was first formed.

Left: THE HAPPY WARRIORS. Cheerful trio of Camel pilots of 28 Squadron; from the left, H B Hudson, G H McLeod, and N C Jones. McLeod was shot down in Camel B2316 on June 8th, 1918 and eventually died in hospital on January 22nd, 1919.

Pilots of 28 Squadron at Grossa, 1918. Second from the right, front row is Captain Stan Stanger, MC.

Cooper bombs were dropped by the Camels. Next day clouds and driving rain interfered with all low-level flying operations to a great extent, but this rain proved to be the final factor in halting the Austrian drive. Filling the upper reaches of the Piave, the rain transformed the waters of the river into a swirling torrent which bore down on the Austrian pontoon bridges and literally swept all before it in the early hours of June 18th. By noon that same day a British reconnaissance report stated that all but two of the bridges were gone, swept towards the sea. This 'act of God', as official histories term the event, sparked off an Italian counter-attack against Austrian troops now trapped west of the Piave, and by June 20th these were retreating slowly towards the river. By June 23rd the Austrian withdrawal had become a full retreat, and the whole available RAF strength was used to assist Italian bombing sorties in harassing the enemy. At one point 44 Camels were airborne and engaged in low-level strafing, bombing and harrying the estimated 70,000 Austrian troops stranded west of the river Piave. The result was inevitable. More than 20,000 Austrians were taken prisoner alone — the Austrian offensive had been decisively beaten back.

As June 1918 petered out ground activity was restricted to a series of localised Italian attacks with limited objectives, but air-to-air activity rose again to its former pitch. By then Allied air supremacy was an established fact, with the Camels as unrivalled masters of their domain. Nevertheless, Austrian fighter pilots continued to offer tough opposition on occasion. On July 12th, in the early morning, Captain C.E. Howell and Lieutenant A. Rice-Oxley from 45 Squadron were climbing for an offensive patrol near Mount Tomba when they spotted a mixed batch of 10 Austrian aircraft approaching from the direction of Feltre. Edging round into the glare of the sun, both Camel pilots attacked, and Howell's first burst tore the lower right wing off the leading Albatros scout. He then destroyed a Phönix Scout in flames. At that moment five Austrian Berg D. scouts dropped out of the sun to join the fray, one of which fastened on Howell's tail. Reversing the position, Howell fired at pointblank range and saw the Berg spin away, pouring smoke. His Camel was immediately beset by four other Austrian scouts, one of which Howell sent down apparently out of control. Joining up with Rice-Oxley (who claimed two victims from this combat later), Howell helped disperse the persistent Austrians; at which point four Italian scouts (two Hanriots and two Spads) led by Italy's leading (living) 'ace', Silvio Scaroni appeared on the scene and proceeded to attack the Austrians. Shooting a Berg off Howell's tail, Scaroni was jumped by a Phönix D III and badly wounded; eventually crashing and being hospitalised for the rest of the war. An Italian Spad shot at an Austrian scout which fell apart in mid-air, before the Allied scouts combined to clear the air of the remaining enemy.**

Only four days later 45 Squadron's popular commander Major A.M. 'Bunny' Vaucour, MC was killed in a tragic case of mis-identification. Flying Camel D8102 on a lone patrol, Vaucour was attacked from behind by an Italian scout and shot down in flames. On July 31st another 45 Squadron pilot, Captain 'Jack' Cottle in Camel D8237, 'D', claimed an 'Albatros' as destroyed, and post-war publications have always credited his victim as being the noted 23-victory 'ace', Oberleutnant Frank Linke-Crawford, who died that same day, crashing at Guia on the Piave. In fact Cottle's victim was almost certainly Feldwebel Acs of Flik 60J and was a Phönix Scout, a design very similar in configuration to the Albatros; while Linke-Crawford died in a Berg D.I. Scout, 115.32, in flames after being shot down by an Italian fighter. Cottle chalked up another success exactly one month later on August 31st when, with two other Camels, he led an attack on six Albatri from Flik 3J escorting a two-seater over Mount Cismon. No less than five scouts were claimed by the Camel trio; three by Cottle and one each by Captain M.R. James and Lieutenant R.G.H. Davies.

** F/n: It should be noted that the claims described here are based only on the RAF pilots' combat reports. Controversy still rages as to the *actual* results of this noted combat.

Camel 'P' of 66 Squadron, trestled into flying attitude during normal daily servicing for ground checks.

PRISONER. Camel B2455, 'X' of 28 Squadron, in which Lt E G Forder was brought down intact on May 11th, 1918 by the noted Austrian 'ace' Oberleutnant Frank Linke-Crawford. Seen here on the Austrian aerodrome at Feltre.

HARMONISATION. B4609, 'F' of 45 Squadron having its Vickers guns harmonised and fire-tested at a makeshift stop butt. This Camel was serving with 28 Squadron by July 1918, and crashed on July 29th, injuring its pilot, Lt A T Wiltshire.

Not all Camel losses were due to enemy action. 28 Squadron's pilots in particular appear to have been extraordinarily lucky in experiencing various flying accidents without fatal results. As on July 12th when Captain T.F. Williams and Lieutenant G.C. Constandurous set out on a free-lance hunt along the Swiss border but found no opponents. On the return journey both Camels dropped low to fly over Lake Garda as an exercise in sheer high spirits to see how low they could get. Williams suddenly had a feeling that he might be just a bit *too* low and instinctively pulled back on his control column — leaving two parallel lines across the still waters of the lake where his wheels had skimmed the surface. Constandurous was not so quick to react to the danger. His Camel sank too low, bucked violently and tossed him out of his cockpit yards ahead of his aircraft. Kicking off his knee-length fur flying boots, the unlucky Constandurous swam back to the wreckage of his Camel but this quickly sank. William dropped his kapok seat cushion to 'Connie' and then hailed a small boat about four miles away. Constandurous had to keep afloat in his water-logged Sidcot suit for 40 minutes before finally being rescued by the rowing boat. Williams' luck held good two days later when a near-miss by anti-aircraft fire shattered a main wing spar and ruptured his petrol tank, flooding the cockpit with fuel. By sheer skill and good judgment Williams managed to glide through the gorge of Brenta and reach safety behind Allied lines. On July 19th he had an even narrower escape from death when, as he was about to dive on a small formation of enemy aircraft, his engine simply disintegrated. Again he reached safety by a skilful glide. Tom Williams flew his last operational sortie with 28 Squadron on July 27th and shot down an Austrian two-seater which glided straight into the side of a mountain north-east of Gallio and exploded in flames. With a credited total of 13 victories, he then left Italy and returned to England.

The 'star turn' (in contemporary RAF vernacular) of 28 Squadron was the Canadian Clifford M. McEwen, who had been an original member of the unit's formation and remained with 28 for the whole of his operational career. On July 20th, 1918 McEwen destroyed a Brandenburg two-seater for his 24th credited victory, and added three more to this total by the end of the war; a record which made him 28 Squadron's highest-scoring pilot within the unit. Other squadron 'aces' included Captain John Mitchell (10 victories), Captain Stan Stanger (9), Captain P. Wilson (8), and Captain J.E. Hallonquist (5, plus shares in two others). One pilot who joined 28 Squadron on August 5th gained no victories in Camels but achieved international fame after the war. He was Lieutenant H J L 'Bert' Hinkler, an Australian, who had served in the RNAS throughout the war in a non-commissioned capacity, but finally achieved his ambition to become a pilot. Hinkler's post-1918 career in record-making long distance flying needs no embellishment here.

The general pace of air fighting over the Italian front eased during September, and on September 12th the squadron flew its final sorties in Italy. Five days later orders were received transferring 45 Squadron to France, there to be attached to the newly-created Independent Force. The squadron finally departed from Italy on September 20th; having claimed a total of 142 enemy aircraft destroyed or brought down in Italy, for the loss of only six Camels. The remaining Camel units, 28 and 66 Squadrons, were based respectively at Sarcedo and St Pietro-in-Gu by the end of September, but moves were already afoot for a 'final' Italian land offensive. By the beginning of October bombing raids had begun to assume greater importance in view of these forthcoming operations. Such raids were made in relatively heavy strength, with the first such sortie being flown on October 4th when 26 Camels from both squadrons bombed and strafed an Austrian flying school at Campoformido. During the course of the raid the Camels dropped ten 40lb phosphor bombs and 77 Cooper (25lb) bombs; obtaining at least 22 direct hits on buildings and sheds, and destroying ten aircraft on the ground. Three other enemy aircraft were destroyed in combats during the Camels' return flight. On the following day 22 Camels released 62 bombs on another flying school at Egna and created heavy damage.

ARCHIE DAMAGE. The shattered engine cowling of a 28 Squadron Camel bears witness to the lucky escape from death by its pilot during a ground-strafing mission. Nearest to the cowling, in Naval cap, is Lieutenant Herbert John Louis Hinkler, DSM—more familiarly known as 'Bert'—who in the post-1918 years became internationally famed for his many long-distance record flights and other aspects of flying.

LAST FIGHT. B7167, 'S' of 66 Squadron, brought down in Austrian territory on October 22nd, 1918 (Lt J M Kelley, PoW). On that date some of 66 Squadron's Camels carried a modified form of 45 Squadron's white dumb-bell unit marking, in an attempt to 'cover up' the recent withdrawal of 45 Squadron from the Italian Front.

An almost unique experience occurred to Captain Stanger of 28 Squadron on October 17th. Leading a voluntary patrol of three Camels over Conegliano, Stanger suffered a bout of dizziness — he had only recently returned from a spell in hospital with 'Mediterranean Fever' — and therefore shut off his engine and started gliding west. Within seconds of turning back he fainted and only regained partial consciousness when about 100 feet over a large field. Landing more by instinct than judgment, Stanger vaguely realised that he must be in enemy-occupied territory and his first thought was to destroy his Camel. Instead he decided to attempt a take-off and, removing his fur boots to use as wheel chocks, he finally got the Camel's engine running again. By now several Austrian soldiers had appeared at one end of the field and were running towards him. Scrambling into his cockpit Stanger began take-off as the leading runner was only ten yards away, and managed to get airborne without further trouble. Still dizzy, Stanger made for Castello di Godega airfield and landed — then promptly fainted again.

Preparations for the proposed Allied offensive were almost complete by the third week of October, and all Allied air units were told to concentrate on destruction of Austrian observation kite balloons in order to preserve secrecy of Allied intentions. This the aircraft did with great success, destroying seven balloons and damaging many others within 48 hours. A move by 28 Squadron from Sarcedo to Limbraga on October 25th brought the unit to the forefront of operations during the opening stages of the land offensive. The purpose of the offensive was to gain footholds on the east banks of the river Piave — a formidable task considering the river's 1½-miles width. The two Camel squadrons were tasked with low-level disruption of enemy troop movements and communications, although air fighting continued spasmodically during such sorties. The Allied master plan was accomplished within four days and, by October 30th, the Austrian armies were in headlong retreat; harried and gunned throughout the hours of daylight by constant air patrols. Flying from first light until dusk the Camel pilots virtually 'lived' in the air above the enemy — pausing only for fresh fuel, bombs and ammunition between sorties. Targets for the ubiquitous Camel pilots were plentiful and widely varied, and from November 1st to 3rd the reign of aerial destruction continued without let-up. Retreating and demoralised masses of infantry were decimated by bombs and machine gun fire, trains wrecked, road transports destroyed or disrupted. The swiftness of the Allied advance was such that many cases occurred of Austrian aircraft returning blissfully to their airfields found these occupied by Italian or British troops. The end to the slaughter came at 1500 hours on November 4th, when an armistice was signed and all hostilities officially ceased.

During the final offensive units of the RAF set up a remarkable record. Almost 20,000lb of bombs had been dropped and more than 51,000 rounds fired, all in the course of 283 offensive sorties. In the air at least nine Austrian aircraft and seven kite balloons had been destroyed, while dozens of others had been sent down out of control or severely damaged. The cost to the RAF had not been light. 28 Squadron alone lost eleven Camels, the pilots of four being officially listed as 'Missing' and the remaining seven prisoners of war, albeit briefly.

The final tally of the Camel squadrons' part in the whole Italian struggle was impressive. From December 1917 to November 1918 Nos 28, 45 and 66 Squadron had claimed a total of no less than 443 enemy aircraft destroyed or conquered. With their war at an end, and the larger conflict in France in its last days, 28 and 66 Squadrons did not remain long in Italy. 28 Squadron moved back to Sarcedo on November 5th, but in February 1919 was shipped home to England at only cadre strength and stationed at its original formation station, Yatesbury, under the aegis of 28th Wing, 7 Group, RAF. After further moves to Leighterton and Eastleigh, 28 Squadron was officially disbanded at Eastleigh on January 20th, 1920. Remaining at St Pietro-in-Gu until March 1919, 66 Squadron, reduced to cadre strength, joined Squadron 28 at Yatesbury. A further move to Leighterton almost immediately followed and here the squadron was officially disbanded on October 25th, 1919.

Captain Matthew Frew, DSO, MC, highest-scoring Camel pilot of 45 Squadron, who remained in the RAF as a career, and eventually retired as Air Vice-Marshal Sir Matthew Frew, KBE, CB, DSO, MC, AFC. He died in May 1974.

CAMEL DUO. Lieutenants H M Moody (left) and R J Brownell, of 45 Squadron, about to leave on a fighting patrol from Istrana, January 1918. Both are wearing the standard issue Sidcot, fleece-lined flying overall suits.

Captain Jack Cottle, DFC of 45 Squadron.

B5401, 'E' of 28 Squadron; a Camel which had served previously with 44 Squadron.

ART-WORK. Lieutenant Masters standing alongside Camel B2407, 'R' of 45 Squadron. The upright stroke of the 'R' has been fashioned in the shape of a (lady's?) leg . . .

MASTER AND STEED. Major W G Barker, DSO, MC, commander of 139 Squadron, and his 'private' aircraft, Camel B6313. By this time Barker had extended 139's double white hoops to four white, interspaced with black, hoops; and added a crimson heart, pierced by a white arrow on the fin. Visible here, attached to the right-hand Vickers gun muzzle is Barker's private mascot—a red devil thumbing its nose in derision. The customary rank streamers were not attached, B6313 being the only Camel on the squadron.

RUNNING-UP. Barker prepares for take-off in B6313. At right is the tail of Bristol F2b D8072, 139 Squadron. As evident here, Barker was by now recording his claimed combat victories as a tally of white marks on each forward interplane strut.

On September 29th, 1918, George Barker took up B6313 for its last operational flight, prior to his posting to England next day. In deference to his fighting record, before B6313 was transferred to No. 7 Aircraft Park for dismantling on October 2nd, Barker was permitted to retain any personal souvenirs from his aircraft. Amongst other items, Barker selected his mascot — a sheet-metal figure, cut in profile, of a red devil thumbing its nose in derision, which had been affixed to the muzzle of his right-hand Vickers gun. It was this same mascot which he later attached to the guns of Sopwith Snipe E8102 in which he fought an epic battle against superior odds on October 27th, 1918 in France and earned the supreme award of a Victoria Cross for his courage.

The ultimate state of Camel B6313 immediately prior to its dismantling reflected the continuing modification put in hand at George Barker's personal preference. The most obvious refinement was the widening of the upper wing centre-section cut-out for better upward visibility from the cockpit; this being extended to include removal of all fabric covering to the trailing edge wire of the centre-section. Other external modifications included four fretting slots cut symmetrically in the face of the engine cowling to assist cooling of the rotary engine in the thin air above the Austrian hills and mountains. A particular idiosyncrasy of Barker's was his refusal to use the standard Aldis sight for his guns. Instead he had two flat steel bars made and affixed respectively across the muzzles and breeches of his Vickers guns. The rear bar had a Vee-notch cut centrally, aligned with a metal bead on the muzzle-bar — virtually a normal rifle sight arrangement. In keeping with Barker's somewhat extrovert character, B6313 was marked progressively in various bright colour schemes. While with 28 Squadron it carried the normal unit marking, a large white square to the rear of the fuselage roundels, and a figure '1' and small 'c' forward of each roundel, indicating No. 1 of C Flight. The white square was also carried above the starboard upper wing, and a '1' on the port upper wing, inboard of the roundels. At that stage the upper wing centre-section was of standard size, but Barker added a small white 'spinner' to the propeller boss, and had the fabric wheel disc covers doped in white.

During his sojourn with 66 Squadron B6313 remained normally marked, but on transfer to command of 139 Squadron Barker proceeded to embellish his Camel. At first he had the squadron's unit markings of two white three-inch wide bands just to the rear of the fuselage roundels, but extended these to four such bars carried around the rear fuselage. He then added a private insigne of a blood-red heart, pierced by a white arrow, applied to each side of the fin; and painted the small, snub propeller bos-spinner in red. As one of Barker's pilots said of him, 'He liked a show', and this may account for some of 139 Squadron's Bristol P2b's having their initial two-bar marking extended to a series of 12 parallel white bars, interspaced by black bars, stretching from the fuselage roundel to the fin. With its stumpier fuselage, B6313 could only accommodate seven such white 'hoopings', and these resulted in over-doping the fuselage serial number. In this form, the fin marking of heart and arrow re-doped and became 'reversed'. One other personal marking of Barker's was the recording of his victory tally in the form of small white flashes painted on each front interplane strut. Photographic evidence confirms that this tally reached at least 37 flashes, but may have been higher before the Camel was finally dismantled.

In its year of war flying B6313, with Barker at the controls, had been responsible for at least 33 enemy aircraft destroyed, nine kite balloons destroyed (seven of these being shared with another Camel), and a further six aircraft sent down completely out of control. No other individual Camel, or indeed any other aircraft of any nation, surpassed this operational record during 1914-18 — B6313 was the 'King'.

Sopwith F.1 Camel, B6313 in its final, fully modified state, in September 1918.

At this time the upper wing centre-section cut-out had been greatly enlarged, even to stripping the fabric back to the trailing edge wire. The engine cowling had been neatly slotted for extra cooling of the engine. The rear fuselage white/black hooping had now been extended, and the fin insignia of heart and arrow reversed. It should be noted also that at no time did George Barker fit a standard Aldis gun sight (see text). Well evident in the frontal aspects are Barker's victory tallymarks on the interplane struts.

CAMEL 'KINGS' (pictorial only)

OFF TO THE WAR. Pilots of 65 Squadron at Wye, Kent in October 1917, prior to 'joining the war' in France. Standing from left: 2/Lt Marshall; Lt Balfour; 2/Lt Brenridge; Lt Pitt; 2/Lt Cutbill; Maj J C Cunningham (OC); Capt L S Weedon; Capt T Withington; Lt Harrison; Lt Scott. Seated, from left, Lt Keller; Lt Gordon; Lt Cocks; Lt Morrison; 2/Lt Rosenthal; Lt Symonds; Lt Wigg; 2/Lt G M Knocker. Of these men, four were killed in action, four others became prisoners of war, and several were wounded in combat.

Camel captains of 80 Squadron prior to flying to France. Standing, from left: Lt Welch; 2/Lt V S Bennett; Lt Oldridge; Lt Brown; Maj V D Bell (OC); Capt Hall; Capt H A Whistler; 2/Lt Gardner; Lt R A Preston. Seated, from left: 2/Lt A A Chadwick; 2/Lt Murray; 2/Lt Milligan; 2/Lt Holt; Lt Potter.

FROM DOWN UNDER. Australian Camel pilots of 4(AFC) Squadron at Clairmarais on June 16th, 1918. Centre figure is the leading Aussie 'ace', Captain Arthur Cobby, DSO, DFC.

61

A motley mixture of uniforms displayed by the pilots of 208 Squadron in late 1918. Seated centre is the unit commander, Major Chris Draper, DSC; while at his left elbow is Captain W E G ('Pedro') Mann, and on his right Captain J B White. Photo taken at Donstiennes, near Charleroi.

Officers of 6(N) Squadron. Far right, standing, is Lieutenant (later, Major) Chris Draper, DSC, who, in 1918, commanded 208 Squadron RAF.

FIGHTING COCKS. Camel pilots of 43 Squadron. From left: G A Lingham; T Purdey (Recording Officer); H Daniel, M.C.; Capt C King, MC; G D Daly, May 1918. King, Daniel and Lingham claimed a total of 34 victories between them in Camels.

Captain Frank Grainger Quigley, DSO, MC, the high-scoring Canadian of 70 Squadron, who died, ironically, of influenza on October 20th, 1918 on his return to England from a period of leave in Canada. Photo taken when Quigley was serving with 9 Squadron RFC prior to joining 70 Squadron.

Major Robert John Orten Compston, DSC, DFC who served with 8(N) Squadron (Camels) and in 1918 commanded 40 Squadron (SE5A's). Rejoining the RAF in WW2, he rose to Wing Commander rank. He died on January 28th, 1962.

Captain John Trollope of 43 Squadron, who was the first RFC pilot to claim six victories in one day's combat operations.

Major Charles Dawson Booker, DSC, another 8(N) pilot, who rose to command of 201 Squadron before his death in August 1918.

FIGHTING LEADER. Captain Henry Winslow Woollett, DSO, MC, seated in the cockpit of his Camel D6402, 'S' of 43 Squadron. Just below the cockpit rim is Woollett's personal insigne.

FIGHTING CANUCK. Squadron Commander Lloyd Breadner, DSC, who rose to become Air Marshal, CB, DSC, Air Officer-in-Chief RCAF overseas in World War Two.

Major Raymond Collishaw, DSO, DSC, DFC, who served in 13(N), 3(N), and commanded 203 Squadron. Pictured here when OC 47 Squadron in Russia, 1919-20. Remaining in the RAF, Canadian-born Collishaw became Air Vice-Marshal, CB, DSO, OBE, DSC, DFC, and died on September 29th, 1976.

Captain William L Jordan, DSC of 8(N) Squadron.

Captain Donald R MacLaren, DSO, MC, DFC who joined 46 Squadron initially and remained with this unit until November 1918, by which time he was commanding officer of the squadron. Born in Canada, of Scottish descent, MacLaren was a leading figure in the post-1918 development of Canadian aviation.

Captain Arthur Gould Lee, MC of 46 Squadron. He later rose to become Air Vice-Marshal, RAF, and on retirement from the Service became a successful author.

Captain Leonard H Slatter, DSC, DFC of 213 Squadron. After the war Slatter commanded, various fighter squadrons of the RAF, and in 1926 was OC RAF High Speed Flight at Felixstowe. Rising to senior rank in WW2, he died in 1961.

Captain Arthur Roy Brown, DSC of 209 Squadron, whose 13 officially accredited victories included the German 'Ace of aces', Rittmeister Manfred von Richthofen; although controversy still rages as to the actual conqueror of the famed 'Red Baron'.

Lt-Colonel William George Barker, VC, DSO, MC, who gained the bulk of his victories in Camel B6313. Killed in a flying accident on March 12th, 1930 at Ottawa, Canada.

Lieutenant David Sinton Ingalls, DSC, DFC, an American naval pilot who flew with 213 Squadron RAF in 1918 and was credited with eight victories. He eventually became a Rear Admiral, USNR.

Captain Ronald Sykes, DFC of 3(N) and 201 Squadrons.

Lieutenant Harold F Stackard in the cockpit of Camel, MAUDE II of 9(N) Squadron, at Furnes, mid-1917.

Excellent view of the cockpit and guns of a Camel. The hump fairing has been removed, disclosing the gun breeches, ammunition chutes (central between guns). Inside the cockpit can be seen the spade-grip top of the control column and 'blip' switch. The non-standard, small windscreen is noteworthy.

A closer view of a Camel cockpit, and the padded back blocks of the twin Vickers .303 machine guns. Between the guns is the rear clamp for an Aldis gun sight (not fitted here).

FROM THE COCKPIT

What was it like to fly in a Camel? It is a curious fact that despite the wealth of published works in which Camels and their exploits have been described or mentioned since 1918, relatively few include authentic, first-hand accounts of what it really meant to pilot a Camel under training conditions or in the cut and thrust of daily combat. Too much of such published material has been hearsay, legend, or at best second-hand information by latter-day historians. Of the men who actually flew the Camel, very few have survived the passage of years to the present day (1977); although in recent years several such men have left behind them excellent autobiographies giving at least a glimpse of contemporary conditions and impressions of the heroic hears 1916-18. One pilot who knew the Camel intimately is Captain Ronald Sykes, DFC, who flew Camels with Nos 9 (N), 201 and 203 Squadrons, flying and fighting in the company of such noted Camel experts as Raymond Collishaw, Leonard Rochford, 'Sam' Kinkead, Roy Brown and many others. And though he has never publicised the fact, Ronald Sykes was an 'ace' in his own right. Based on his contemporary original notes and log book, Sykes has recorded the following descriptions — virtually a set of 'Pilot's Notes' — on how to fly a Camel; then expands on various facets of the Camel when flown in the operational context. In the main these notes relate to the 150 hp BR1-engined version used extensively by most RNAS units, though the general procedures for take-off, cockpit checks et al are representative of most Camel variants.

Climb up and sit on the hump over the petrol tank just behind the cockpit and slide forward into the seat (under the plane), slipping your toes under the straps of the rudder bar. Take a look at all control surfaces while moving the stick and rudder bar. See that both magnetic switches are off and that the petrol fine-adjustment lever is closed. Turn the petrol tap ON to 'Main Tank'. Turn on the cock behind the air pump and hand-pump up to 1½lb/sq in; at this pressure the relief valve should blow off. Turn the cock OFF. Open the petrol fine-adjustment by pushing the short lever for about one-half of its travel.

Answer the air mechanic's call of 'Switches Off'; 'Petrol On'; Suck in. While the propeller is being pulled round, move the long lever on the quadrant (controlling the barrel throttle-valve) a little way forward until a sucking, gurgling noise is heard as the petrol and air are drawn through the barrel throttle in the hollow crankshaft into the rotating crankcase. (The mixture passes through the crankcase and up the induction pipes to the overhead inlet valves.) While the propeller is being turned round, the oil pump will be drawing pure castor oil from the oil tank and forcing it to the crankshaft bearings, timing gears, master and slave big-ends, and cylinder walls; all of which are scoured by the petrol vapour, the castor oil being insoluble in petrol. Meanwhile the pilot fastens his waist belt, winds his muffler over his nose and mouth, and secures it by his helmet chin-strap. After several turns of the engine the propeller is turned back to a position about '10 o'clock'; then the mechanic shouts, 'Contact'. The pilot puts both switches ON, the petrol fine-adjustments lever nearly right back, the throttle half-open and replies, 'Contact.' The mechanic pulls the propeller down smartly; and in turn has his arm or belt pulled hard by the rigger to get him clear of the propeller as the engine fires.

DASHBOARD. Main instrumentation in a Camel. Both Vickers guns have been removed, and in foreground is the control column spadegrip top.

TAXYING

One of the pleasing features of the BR1 engine in comparison with earlier makes is that it responds normally to the throttle and does not require 'blipping', although a blip-switch is provided in the spade-handle of the joystick. So the initial engine run-up to give about 1,050 revs can be done by opening the throttle and petrol fine-adjustment lever together; the stick is, of course, held right back and the rigger lies over the fuselage to help keep the tail down. Then 'Chocks Away'. Push the stick forward and put on some rudder; give a burst of engine to take the weight off the tail skid and blow the tail round. Visibility forward is nil (owing to the twin Vickers guns and Aldis Sight between them), so look out sideways and, if all is clear, turn into the line of vision. Once the Camel is moving freely there seems to be a tendency for the tail to bounce up, so keep the stick back while running on the grass. Check the windsock direction and turn into wind.

TAKE-OFF

Check for 1½lb/sq in. air pressure in the pipe to the air space in the main petrol tank; this can be corrected by adjusting the relief valve or by pumping air with the hand pump near to the right l.and. Look to see that no other machine is coming in to land; pull down your mask goggles; open the throttle wide and simultaneously move the fine-adjustment lever just past the half-way position on the quadrant, when your ear will tell you that the mixture is correct and the engine firing evenly. While the engine revs are rising, kick on plenty of left rudder to prevent a swing to the right. As speed increases push the stick forward and get the tail skid off the ground, high enough to give some visibility over the engine cowling. As the pressure against the stick rises, let it come back until the wheels leave the surface and the Camel flies off. Against a wind of about Force 3 or 4, this will be at about 45 knots in approximately 150 yards with full tank (24 gallons in main, 4 gallons in emergency gravity tanks) and two 500-round belts of .303 ammunition.

The Camel will not fly itself hands-off, and when the wheels leave the ground it will be tail-heavy with the full load of petrol in the tank behind you; you will also find it sluggish on the ailerons and too near the stall, so gently push the stick forward an inch or two and fly parallel to the ground with the wheels two or three feet clear of it. The speed quickly rises to 100 knots and the controls become very sensitive. Let the stick come back an inch or two and you will put the Camel into a steady climb of 1,000 ft/minute at 60 knots. Throttle and fine-adjustment lever must now be pulled back slightly; your ear will note the improvement in the tone of the engine as rpm come back to the figure marked 1,250 maximum. During the climb it is necessary to pull back the fine-adjustment lever at every 1,000 feet at least, otherwise the mixture becomes too rich and advertises the fact by leaving a trail of dark smoke behind, clearly visible for one's critics to observe!

CHARACTERISTICS

Our operational Camels are adjusted by our riggers to be slightly tail-heavy at take-off with full tanks; thus at the end of a 2½-hours flight, with most petrol gone, they will be slightly nose-heavy when coming in to land. During the middle period of such a flight no force is required on the stick to keep in level flight and the Camel will fly (momentarily) hands-off; but the weight of the stick usually carries it slowly to one side — without dihedral on its top plane the machine has little inherent stability about its rolling axis. At all speeds between 70 knots and 150 knots the control response is precise and delightful, although the elevator becomes much more sensitive at 150 knots. Stalling speed in level flight without war load is around 42 knots. Prior to an engine-off stall the aileron response becomes very poor, the machine begins to sink, then kicks up its tail; but if the controls are kept central the machine will fall nose-first, accelerating fairly slowly until at 60 knots it will again respond normally to all controls.

Pull up into a stall and apply the usual encouragement from the rudder; the Camel will then cartwheel over and then flick into a spin, which with the stick held right back will be a fast one. Centralise the controls and after about four more turns the machine will come out of the spin. It can be forced out more quickly by applying opposite rudder and pushing the stick forward briskly, though this does not always have the desired result.

Captain Samuel Marcus Kinkead, DSO, DSC, DFC, of 201 Squadron, seen here in the cockpit of a 47 Squadron Camel in Russia, 1920. Kinkead later became a member of the 1928 RAF High Speed Flight, preparing for the Schneider Trophy Races, and was killed during a practice run off Calshot on March 12th. He is buried in nearby Fawley village churchyeard.

Major G W Murlis-Green, DSO, MC, OC 44 Squadron, takes off from Hainault Farm, Essex in a modified Camel. Note twin Lewis machine guns mounted above the extra-width cut-out centre-section of the upper wing, and additional wing root cut-outs on both lower wings.

NIGHT FIGHTERS

The introduction of the Camel to operational service coincided with a new phase in the German air attacks on the United Kingdom. Apart from a few isolated aircraft sorties the main raiders during the years 1914-16 had been airships; but on May 25th, 1917 a fresh terror was added to the British civil population's ordeal — long-range Gotha bombers, making their first concerted bombing assault. At that time the motley collection of differing aircraft types employed on Home Defence duties included very few of the latest designs; these being urgently needed on the Western Front. Nevertheless, successes had been achieved by a handful of pilots who had been fortunate to have been in the right place at the right time. The early Gotha attacks were made by day, thus allowing the few Camels then beginning to be issued to Home Defence units to attempt interception — due to its early reputation for being tricky to handle, the Camel was considered too unstable to be flown by night. On Saturday, July 7th, 1917 a total of 24 Gothas set out initially to bomb London, and 95 Home Defence aircraft took off piecemeal to tackle the raiders. Five of those defenders were Camels; Flight Lieutenants C. Draper and Watkins rose from Eastchurch, Lieutenant H.T. Tizard took up B3751, while in B3774 Flight Sub-Lieutenant J.E. Scott closed with one Gotha about 35 miles out to sea and fired nearly 500 rounds into the huge bomber. The Gotha heeled over and dived into the sea — the only recorded German loss for this raid.

On August 12th eleven Gothas attacked coastal towns in south-eastern Kent and were variously engaged by many of the 109 defending aircraft despatched to intercept. Almost 20 of these were Camels and 12 got within firing range — only to suffer gun jams. None claimed a victim. Ten days later the Gothas returned, when ten bombers attacked Dover, Ramsgate and Margate. To engage these raiders 120 Home Defence aircraft eventually took off. In Camel B3844 Flight Sub-Lieutenant E.B. Drake from Westgate made several close attacks on one Gotha without visible result. Squadron Commander C.H. Butler from Manston had his Camel damaged by return fire from a Gotha gunner and was forced to land, but immediately took off again in another Camel, B3843. Closing with a Gotha over Ramsgate, he was forestalled by Flight Lieutenant Arthur F. Brandon in Camel B3834, whose fire damaged the Gotha's starboard engine and caused the bomber to burst into flames. The blazing wreckage fell near Manston, and Brandon was later awarded a Distinguished Service Cross (DSC) for this victory.

By the close of August 1917 the accumulative losses of Gothas — due mainly to landing crashes and technical faults, but in no small measure to the determination of the UK defenders — led the German authorities to use Gothas in night raids rather than by day. Four Gothas undertook a night sortie on September 3rd, attacking objectives around the mouth of the Thames Estuary. Only 16 defending aircraft were sent up to intercept, but these included three Camels from 44 Squadron, piloted by the unit commander Major W. Murlis-Green, Captain Christopher J.Q. Brand and Lieutenant C.C. Banks. Although none of the Camel trio sighted the Gothas their 40-minute sortie finally shattered the theory that Camels could not be flown at night safely. By a curious coincidence, that same night saw two Camels of 70 Squadron in France take off in an attempt to intercept several German night bombers raiding the RFC Depot at St. Omer. 44 Squadron RFC, formed at Hainault Farm, Essex on July 24th, 1917 with Sopwith 1½ Strutters, began receiving Camels in August, and by early September was completely re-equipped with standard F.1 Camels — the first Camel squadron specifically designated for Home Defence duties.

Few facilities were available then at the various airfields to assist night-flying. A crude flare-path was normally provided by two rows of cans filled with petrol soaked rag, lit by hand as required, while aircraft usually carried a Holt flare under each lower wing tip to assist the pilot's vision during landing. This latter device was, understandably, used sparingly by most pilots, who were acutely conscious of the fire hazard to their wood and fabric wings. Inside a Camel cockpit the only additional aid to night fliers was a crude form of instrument lighting. The problems associated with

B3834, individually named WONGO-BONGO, at the RNAS War School, Manston, and in which FSL A F Brandon destroyed a Gotha raider on August 22nd, 1917. In background are a Sopwith Triplane and a Sopwith 1½ Strutter.

Eighteen F.1 Camels of 44 Squadron at Hainault Farm, 1918. It should be noted that a majority were standard Camels, with normal cockpit and armament.

Rear view of some of 44 Squadron's standard F.1 Camels, each bearing the single white hoop Flight marking.

Standard F.1 Camel of 44 Squadron, fitted out and marked for night flying. Holt flares are attached under each lower wing tip, while the white circles in wing cockades are doped over. As an individual pilot's whimsy, a cartoon terrier dog is 'leashed' to the small fuselage cockade. Note crescent moon painted above hangar door in background.

WINTER SCENE. A 44 Squadron pilot prepares for take-off from a snow-covered Hainault Farm.

B9175, '5' of 44 Squadron, fitted with under-wing Holt flares. It previously served with 3 Squadron in France.

gun-sighting in total darkness were investigated early in 1917. The standard ring and bead sights for day use had already proved useless by night, and in March 1917 Sergeant A.E. Hutton of 39 Squadron invented the first practical solution to the overall problem. By having the bead sight pierced with a small hole, and placing a red electric bulb in its stem, and similarly piercing holes in the three extremities of the Vee-sight with internal green bulbs; Hutton had produced a simple but workable illuminated gun sighting arrangement. In December 1917 this sight was replaced by the Neame sight; virtually the same arrangement with the additional modification of a ring-sight graduated to give automatic estimation of target range by pre-sized rings.

The pioneer night Camel flights by 44 Squadron on September 3rd, 1917 quickly led to the type being regarded as the most effective night fighter, and during the following weeks Camels were prominent in the many interceptions made against marauding Gothas and airships. Of these, however, none met with any positive success until the night of December 18th, 1917. On that occasion a force of 13 Gothas and a single 'Giant', R.12, bombed London and several east coast towns with little opposition; with only three of the 47 Home Defence aircraft airborne making any form of contact with the raiders. One of these contacts was by Major Murlis-Green who caught a Gotha near London and put its starboard engine out of action. The Gotha subsequently ditched in the sea near Folkestone, Kent and was actually destroyed by a self-destruct device while being salvaged by a trawler. The first unqualified victory in aerial combat by night between aircraft came on the night of January 25th, 1918, when seven Gothas and the 'Giant' R.39 again attacked London and coastal resorts in Kent. Two Camel pilots from 44 Squadron, Captain G.H. Hackwill and Lieutenant C.C. Banks, caught one Gotha near Wickford, Essex and their combined fire brought the bomber down at Frund's Farm, near Wickford.

Encouraging as such successes were, a majority of night sorties by defending aircraft continued to be fruitless. Even the few contacts made by the Camel pilots were often frustrated by pilots being temporarily blinded by the muzzle flash of their twin Vickers guns on opening fire, causing them to lose sight of the target. To eliminate this hazard a new armament arrangement was quickly incorporated on most Camel units. The Vickers guns were removed and two Lewis guns were mounted above the upper wing centre-section, each attached to a separate Foster rail-mounting, thereby permitting a pilot to fire upwards at an angle of about 45-degrees or directly forward above the upper wing. In order to give the pilot ease of manipulation of the twin-Lewis gun mountings, the cockpit was relocated back in line with the lower wings' trailing edge, and the main petrol tank repositioned in front of the cockpit under the wing centre-section. Such modified Camels, referred to as 'Sopwith Comics', often had enlarged centre section cut-outs to improve upward visibility, while many had an SE5a-type head-rest added at the rear of the cockpit coaming. The problem of muzzle flash was further solved by the RFC Experimental station at Orfordness, which produced effective flash eliminator muzzle attachments for both Vickers and Lewis guns; though few such eliminators appear to have been actually used by Camel units.

The frustration for the night fighter pilots in seldom making even contact with German raiders continued through the early months of 1918; an example being the night of February 17th when 69 HD aircraft were airborne — 22 of these being Camels — and only one indecisive contact was made. The dangers involved in flying by night were emphasised during a raid by five 'Giant' bombers on March 7th. Two of the 42 defending aircraft which took off hoping to intercept were Camels flown by Captain H.C. Stroud of 61 Squadron and Captain A.B. Kynoch of 37 Squadron. In the pitch-black of a moonless night these Camels collided in mid-air, killing both pilots. By this date six HD squadrons had supplemented 44 Squadron by receiving Camels in place of their former BE's, Sopwith 1½ Strutters and other types. At Sutton's Farm, Essex (later retitled Hornchurch) 78 Squadron flew its first night sorites with Camels on September 30th, 1917. At Throwley 112 Squadron began replacing its Sopwith Pups with Camels and, on February 8th, 1918, detached one Flight to Detling as the nucleus of a fresh unit, 143 Squadron. At Bekesbourne, Kent, 50 Squadron commenced re-equipment with Camels in the same month; while two other HD units — 61 Squadron at Rochford, and 37 Squadron at Stow Maries — were each issued with a few Camels to form one Flight within each unit.

Major Christopher Quintin Brand, DSO, MC, DFC, who commanded 112 and 151 Squadrons in succession. A pioneer of night fighting, Brand was knighted post-1918 for other pioneering long-distance flights, and eventually retired as Air Vice-Marshal, KBE, DSO, MC, DFC.

Night fighting Camel's twin Lewis guns, mounted on Foster rail slides, normally worked in unison. Here, the starboard Lewis has been fixed to fire upwards at a 45-degree angle. Each Lewis gun had its own Neame illuminated gun sight.

Major G W Murlis-Green, DSO, MC, who served successively in 17, 44, and 70 Squadrons, commanding both latter units.

Captain G Baker, OC 'B' Flight, 112(HD) Squadron and his Camel, 'Tootsie'; with Air Mechanic Tucker refuelling the main tank.

D6415 of 112(HD) Squadron. Holding the two unit mascot dogs, Tinker and Tip, is Lt A S C Irwin. Note cockades over-doped to eliminate white circles, while main fabric is doped dark green.

Lieutenant Scotcher of 112(HD) Squadron, in the cockpit of 'PIXIE III'. The swastika tail marking was simply a good luck symbol at that period, but the tasteful fuselage patterning in shades of green was unusual.

Contacts with individual German raiders were made in the following few weeks, but the first confirmed victory** was not registered until July 25th, when Captain A.B. Yuille (Camel D6573) spotted a 'Gotha' (sic) just after midnight and made several close attacks. He finally lost sight of his opponent but this was confirmed as crashed in Allied lines later with both engines out of action and a crew member wounded. A clear night on August 1st saw the first 'intruder' sorties by 151's Camels when the German bomber airfields at Estrees and Guizancourt were selected for attack. Captain S. Cockerell arrived over Estrees just as a bomber was landing and promptly released a 25lb Cooper bomb some 50 yards from the German. He then fired 200 rounds at a second bomber, but the immediate extinguishing of all airfield lights prevented him from seeing any results. Captain W.H. Haynes was also roaming over Estrees that night and saw three Gothas approaching the airfield. Dropping his Cooper bombs onto the ground searchlights to dowse these, Haynes attacked the nearest Gotha, only to suffer jams in both guns.

On the following night the Camels returned to Estrees and Guizancourt, led by the squadron commander Christopher Brand who arrived over Guizancourt and remained above the airfield for about 40 minutes. First dropping his bombs on a hangar, Brand then dived on a large, two-seat aircraft about to land and watched his tracers enter the machine'e engine and cockpits. After attacking a second aircraft, Brand completed his sortie by machine gunning hangars and search-lights. Just after Brand left the scene, his place was taken by Captain Cockerell who proceeded to bomb and strafe the landing field. Turning his attention to a twin-engined aircraft coming in to land, Cockerell gave it a long burst at close range and saw his target eventually crash some two miles from the perimeter of the airfield. Christopher Brand was again airborne on the night of August 7th when, in company with one other Camel, he strafed a bomber about to land at Estrees. The German fell away in flames and both Camels then bombed some hangars before returning to base.

Captain A.B. Yuille, in Camel D6573, was flying a regular night patrol on August 10th when his attention was drawn to a German bomber coned by searchlights over Abbeville. Closing under the tail of the huge aircraft — Staaken R.XIV 'Giant', 43/16 — he fired five short bursts and one of the Staaken's engines stopped, and a fire started in its mid-fuselage. Heeling over on one wing, the stricken 'Giant' fell trailing a spume of flames and crashed near Talmas on the British side of the trenches. On the same night Lieutenants C.R.W. Knight and J.H. Summers (B5412) attacked a bomber at 9,000 feet which crashed in flames. Searchlight coning helped Lieutenant A.V. Blenkiron (D9577) to locate an AEG bomber on August 13th. Closing to pointblank range, he fired several crisp bursts and the AEG spun down in flames almost immediately. Again, on August 22nd, the searchlight crews played their part by illuminating a Friedrichshafen G III for Captain Yuille and Lieutenant Knight (D6660). Yuille attacked first but after two brief bursts over-shot his target. Knight closed under the bomber's tail and, after firing 50 rounds from each of his Vickers guns, saw the machine burst into flames and fall into some British trenches. Yuille received a Distinguished Flying Cross (DFC) shortly afterwards. That same night Lieutenant W. Aitken (D9445) caught a Gotha GVb from *Bogohl* III and shot it down to crash. Two nights later Captain F.C. Broome (D6102) and Lieutenant Knight (D6660) registered confirmed victories; shooting down a Gotha GVb and a Friedrichshafen respectively.

Bad weather conditions brought a lull in night-flying activities during the first two weeks of September 1918, but the night of September 13th proved a hectic one for 151 Squadron's Camel pilots who claimed four victories. Lieutenant E.P, MacKay (F1979) attacked a Friedrich-shafen coned by searchlights just north of Peronne, and his close assault forced the German crew to land in Allied territory where they became prisoners of war. In Camel E5142 Captain Haynes destroyed a twin-engined bomber in flames near Manacourt, and 25 minutes later hit a Friedrich-shafen with two accurate bursts of 50 rounds. The bomber spiralled down within German lines and its end was not seen. A fourth claim, also unconfirmed, was by Lieutenant A.V. Blenkiron who attacked an AEG in the Bapaume area which apparently crashed.

** F/n: In fact, 151's pilots had claimed three victories before this date — on June 28th, and July 6th, but these had not been officially confirmed by RAF authorities.

Pilots of 112(HD) Squadron at Bells Forstal Farm circa June 1918. Major Christopher Brand (OC) is seated centre in the middle row. Second from right, rear row (holding dog) is Lt Tommy Broome, DFC, who later served with Brand in 151 Squadron.

E5165, an F.1 Camel converted for night duties, at the AFC training station Leighterton Its pilot here is the Australian Captain E F 'Tab' Pflaum, a veteran combat pilot who had seen service in France with 4 (AFC) Squadron.

37 Squadron's 'A' Flight pilots at Stow Maries, Essex. From left: Lts Lingard, Foster, Hay, Phillips, and Nichols.

Camels of 143 Squadron at Detling, 1918. Wheel discs were doped in red/white/blue concentric circles.

Though of poor quality, a rare view of a 151 Squadron night-fighter Camel, fitted with underwing Holt flares.

A modified Camel, incorporating the re-located cockpit and fitted with under-wing Holt flares, but without armament. Probably in use for training purposes.

The most successful week of 151 Squadron's brief war service, however, was that of September 16th to 22nd, when eight night bombers fell to the Camels' guns. During the same week the unit moved base to Vignacourt. At 8,000 feet on the night of September 15th Major Brand engaged a Friedrichshafen; his bullets apparently rupturing an engine oil sump because Brand's Camel was liberally sprayed with oil, forcing his to break off the combat. Captain F.C. Broome in D6102 had better luck that night when he attacked a Staaken 'Giant' (R VI, 31/16) coned by searchlights. Closing to minimal range Broome fired more than 500 rounds into the behemoth before it erupted in flames and fell within British lines. Two nights later the squadron claimed three victims, despite a cloudy, overcast night. Major Brand (D6423) spotted a Friedrichshafen illuminated by the faithful searchlight crews and began his attack from close range. The machine almost immediately fell in flames, and then one of its bombs exploded and tore the bomber apart in the air. The second victory belonged to Captain D V Armstrong (C6713) who shot down a Friedrichshafen G III of *Bogohl* VI/8 at Fletre, near Bapaume, while Lieutenant MacKay (F1979) poured 250 rounds into an AEG G V and watched it crash south-east of Estrees-en-Chausee, catching fire on the ground. Three nights later Captain Broome (D6102) fired 100 rounds into an AEG G V which spun away in flames and exploded on impact near Tincourt.

On September 20th/21st Major Brand (D6423) attacked a DFW which, after his attack, zoomed and fell over backwards before disappearing from Brand's vision. This victory was later confirmed by some British infantry who witnessed the DFW's final crash. The following night brought three more victories for 151. First to fall was a Friedrichshafen G IIIa to the guns of Major Brand's Camel, D6423; and later Brand joined forces with Lieutenant J.H. Summers (C6713) to destroy an AEG which crashed near Bourlon. The third victory that night went to Lieutenant A.A. Mitchell (C8277) who dived on an AEG, hit the German's port engine with a burst of 175 rounds, and forced it to crash-land near Cambrai. September 25/26th brought a victory for Lieutenant T.R. Bloomfield in Camel F6084. Patrolling east of Bapaume, he spotted an 'AEG' (sic) and immediately attacked; seeing his fire strike sparks from the machine's starboard engine. The slipstream of his opponent forced the Camel away and he lost sight of his target. Forty minutes later Bloomfield opened fire on a Gotha, damaging its starboard engine and causing a spray of oil to envelop his Camel. Virtually 'blinded' by the oil, Bloomfield was again forced to disengage. Later evidence listed a total of five unidentified enemy aircraft destroyed in the same area, and Bloomfield was credited with '. . . at least one enemy aircraft confirmed destroyed!'

On October 6th came awards of DFC's to Major Brand, and Captains D.V. Armstrong and F.C. Broome for their consistently brilliant work over the past year; and two days later 151 Squadron moved forward to Bancourt airfield in the wake of a retreating German army. From this base on October 28th Lieutenant L.L. Carter (F1887) attacked a 'Gotha' but lost control of his Camel temporarily and lost further contact. On the following night Major Brand had better fortune and claimed his squadron's final victory. Flying his usual Camel, D6423, he spotted a Friedrichshafen at 9,000 feet trapped in a cone of searchlight beam. Diving fast, he fired 230 rounds and the bomber crashed in flames south-east of Etreux. In five months of intensive operations 151 Squadron had claimed at least 21 enemy aircraft destroyed, five more probably destroyed, and several damaged or indecisive — all with a single squadron casualty.

Returning to the UK after the November 1918 armistice, 151 Squadron was stationed briefly at Gullane in Scotland before being disbanded on September 10th, 1919. Tragically, one of its finest exponents of flying a Camel, Captain D'Urban Victor Armstrong, DFC — whose ability to aerobat Camels to their limits had made him a legend in his own lifetime — did not survive to see England or his native South Africa again. On November 13th 1918 he took up Camel C6713 for a local flight and over the airfield commenced to stunt as only he could. The Camel never recovered from a near-vertical spin and dove straight into the earth at full power.

A second Camel night fighter unit, 152 Squadron, with an identical role to 151, arrived in France on October 22nd, 1918, but saw no active operations before the Armistice. On the night that 152 Squadron arrived in France a pilot from an American Camel unit scored a victory for which he was never officially credited. Major Harold Hartney, commanding the 185th Aero Squadron, USAS, on a night patrol in Camel F1445 attacked a 'Gotha' without visible results as to its fate. Hartney made no claim officially, but confirmation of his victory came later when its wreckage was discovered by advancing Allied troops.

COLOURFUL CAMELS (pictorial only)

Captain Clifford M McEwen, MC, DFC of 28 Squadron poses beside a highly decorated D8239, at Florence, early 1919. Check pattern is thought to be red/white.

Captain P Wilson, another member of 28 Squadron, with an unidentified Camel at Florence, early 1919.

F4017, dazzle-doped in geometrical shapes in red/white/blue/black, which belonged to 204 TDS, Eastchurch in late 1918. In the air-to-air view, it is being flown by an instructor, Captain L P Coombes, an ex-member of 10(N) Squadron.

When 3(N) Squadron was detached from France to Walmer, Kent for a two-months' rest and recuperation on November 4th, 1917, its pilots took the opportunity to mark their Camels in outlandish dope schemes, as witnessed here by B3858. By mid-1918 this particular Camel was serving with 209 Squadron, and was the machine in which Second Lieutenant H R Frank was lost in action on July 4th, 1918.

CAMOUFLAGE. D6402, 'S' of 43 Squadron, the 'personal' Camel of Captain Henry Woollett, who had this patchwork 'camouflage' applied for a series of attacks against German kite balloons. Mistaken for a German in the heat of combat by his own men, Woollett quickly had his Camel re-doped in standard colours!

In Belgian livery. Camel Sc23 and its pilot Tollet.

B7175, usually flown by Captain Leonard H Slatter, of 213 Squadron, and carrying a red/white/blue tricolour band around its rear fuselage. The off-centre wheel disc 'eye' marking was in red/white. Note Slatter's wide, 'wrap-around' form of wind-screen in place of the stan-dard hump fairing; thereby providing immediate access to gun breeches in the event of jams.

Right & Above: Two views of B7380, the 1,000th aeroplane to be produced by the Lincoln firm of Ruston, Proctor & Co. Ltd., and completed on January 4th, 1918. With special permission, this machine was emblazoned with the Behudet (an Egyptian winged sun) in shades of red, white, blue, apple green, blue-grey, and yellow orange. In the second view is Lt Marcus Tyrrell, and colour values are simply a result of the type of film in use.

B6398, 'Cleopatra', in the tasteful livery applied by Captain E L Foot at the Gosport School of Special Flying, late 1918. This Camel had previously served with 201 and 209 Squadrons; in the latter unit being the aircraft in which Captain S T Edwards had brought down Leutnant Hubner of JG1 on May 16th, 1918.

Occasionally, pilots' individual markings took the form of stylized monograms of their name initials, or—as in this view of D9496 of 210 Squadron—of the names of girlfriends or wives. Standing alongside 'DOT' here is Lt John E Berry, at Boissieres aerodrome, near Cambrai, late 1918. Berry claimed two Fokker D VII's in 'DOT', on October 8th and November 10th, 1918 respectively.

Initials of Captain A W Carter of 210 Squadron are artistically applied here to the flanks of D3332; a Camel which served previously with 3(N); 4(N); and 9(N) Squadrons, and achieved a total of at least six victories for its pilots.

An unarmed instructional Camel elaborately marked with an Oriental-styled dragon and snake-biting bird, at a 1918 UK training unit.

F2010, '5' of 70 Squadron at Bickendorf aerodrome, near Cologne in 1919, displaying the three white hoops unit marking of the period. Originally a presentation aircraft, this Camel had been initially titled 'Shanghai Race Club No. 2'; replacing a De Havilland 4 which had borne this inscription.

B5198 of a UK training unit, carrying a camel cartoon on its fin, and checks on fuselage and propeller.

All-white Camels among UK training units were not uncommon. Three examples were (top) E7259, Captain G Malley's machine at 5(AFC) Training Squadron; B5157 of 'F' Flight, Gosport, which had seen previous service as 'M' of 210 Squadron; and C42 of the CFS, Upavon, named somewhat cynically 'The White Feather' and which, on October 24th, 1918, was at the Taranto Depot in the Mediterranean zone of operations. In the latter's case, even the Vickers guns were painted white . . .

A well-publicised but excellent view of 2.F1 N6635, fitted with a 150hp AR1 (later known as BR1) engine.

A standard production 2.F1 Ships Camel, N7136, built by William Beardmore & Co, viewed at Dalmuir on emergence from the factory. In October 1918 this machine was at the Turnhouse naval depot, awaiting allocation.

Whichever the true story of the FS.1/N4, the second prototype N5 has come to be regarded as the real prototype 2F.1. The differences between the standard F.1 and 2F.1 Camels were somewhat greater than most published accounts imply. Although on a similar basic outline and construction as the F.1, the 2F.1 had shorter-span wings (by virtue of a reduced span centre-section), slightly greater lower wing dihedral, narrower wheel track, completely revised armament installation, and centre-section struts of slim steel tubing. The fuselage was constructed in two main sections; the rear ten feet length, including tail assembly, being detachable and 'hinged' for ease of ship stowage and transportation by land. When joined to the forward fuselage, the butt joint was secured by four simple turnbuckles mounted externally, each mounted on a main longeron. On N5 the elevator control cables ran internally for most of the fuselage length, but the later use of internally-stowed air flotation bags in the rear portion of the fuselage necessitated re-routing these cables externally. The guns' arrangement was almost certainly a result of the Admiralty's prime concern with the German airship menace. One Vickers .303 machine gun was mounted in front of the cockpit, synchronised to fire forward through the propeller arc, but a second gun, a Lewis .303, was fixed to fire upwards over the top plane. On N5 this Lewis was apparently fixed directly on the rear spar of the upper wing, in a narrow, straight-sided Vee cut-out at the trailing edge of the centre-section, and inverted. On later production 2F.1's a central upper wing cut-out aperture, similar to those in production F.1's, was incorporated, permitting use of an Admiralty Top Gun Mounting. This device wholly mounted the Lewis above the upper wing, with a Foster-type let-down slide for adjustment of the firing angle and/or reloading magazines.

Even at the earliest stages of the N5 test programme provision had been made for carriage of a wireless transmitter set. Power for this set came from a folding, wind-driven generator on the port side of the fuselage, near the cockpit. Its aerial lead was let out through a tube fairlead under the fuselage. In June 1917 the N5 was subjected to tests with additional armament in the form of eight electrically-ignited Le Prieur rockets, mounted four to each pair of interplane struts — another conscious attempt to combat the Zeppelins. Production of 2F.1's was put in hand on a rather restricted scale; the first order for 50 machines (N6600 - N6649) going to Sopwith's, and deliveries commencing in the autumn of 1917. Eventually a total of 650 'Ships Camels' (the official naval title for 2F.1's) was ordered, although slightly less than half of these orders was later cancelled. The standard engine for the 2F.1 was the 150 hp BR1, but a number of 130 hp Clergets were also used on active service machines. The other major contractor for producing 2F.1's was William Beardmore & Company Ltd, makers of the Beardmore WB III shipboard fighters which the 2F.1's were to replace. The first Beardmore-built 2F.1, N6750, was delivered to the Service on February 20th, 1918.

Experiments in June 1917 had shown the feasibility of RNAS flying boats being towed on lighters behind destroyers, thus extending the functional range of these aircraft for North Sea patrols. It was then suggested that smaller aircraft, such as the 2F.1, could equally be sea-borne using a tiny platform, towed in similar fashion. The pioneer naval pilot, Commander Charles Rumney Samson, promptly undertook testing of this project. Modifying 2F.1, N6623 by fitting a skid undercarriage in place of its normal wheels, Samson used a flat, wooden lighter platform as his 'runway', with parallel wooden troughs from bow to stern to guide the aircraft's skids. On May 30th, 1918 Samson personally undertook the first trial of towed take-off in N6623 — and was lucky to escape drowning. With the lighter making 32 knots, Samson waved to his crew to release the Camel, which proceeded to jump its guide troughs and cartwheeled over the port side of the lighter's bow. With amazing good fortune Samson managed to disentangle himself from the wreckage of the 2F.1 and came to the surface unharmed, where he was quickly retrieved by an attendant whaler. Undismayed by his adventure, Samson immediately pressed for further trials of lighter-borne Camels, and on July 31st Lieutenant Stuart Culley achieved an entirely successful take-off in a 2F.1 fitted with standard wheeled undercarriage. Just ten days later Culley vindicated Samson's faith in the project by taking off in similar fashion and destroying a Zeppelin.

Two views of 2.F1 N6623, with skid undercarriage, aboard a wooden lighter at Felixstowe on May 29th, 1918; the day before
Commander C R Samson's first attempt to
take-off while under tow at sea.

The successful trial flown by Lt Stuart Culley on July 31st, 1918 showing (top) under tow; (centre) the moment of take-off from the lighter; and (bottom) Stuart Culley (standing, in RN uniform) with his 'crew' and another 2.F1 Camel at Felixstowe.

The first naval actions in which 2F.1's figured occurred in June 1918, when Camels from the Australian light cruisers *Sydney* and *Melbourne* took off on June 1st to intercept several German seaplanes protecting an enemy mine-sweeping force. Unfortunately, gun troubles precluded any successful engagements on this occasion. On June 18th further non-productive take-offs were made by Camels from *Galatea* and the aircraft carrier *Furious,* intending to engage some patrolling German aircraft. Two Camels from *Furious* were compelled to ditch in the sea; while *Galatea's* aircraft did not return, having force-landed in Denmark where its pilot was interned. Later the same day two more Camels left the *Furious* to engage a pair of enemy seaplanes attempting to bomb the carrier. Lieutenant G. Heath forced one of the seaplanes down on the sea, where its crew were taken prisoner and the machine destroyed by gunfire from an attendant destroyer.

The aircraft carrier *Furious* was to figure in one of the 2F.1s most spectacular successes. On July 18th, 1918, after several delays due to atrocious weather conditions, seven Camels (of an intended formation of eight originally) took off in two Flights from the forward deck of *Furious,* each loaded with two specially-made 50lb Cooper bombs, and intending to fly 80 miles across open sea to raid the Zeppelin shed complex at Tondern, in Schleswig-Holstein. The first three Camels away, piloted by Captains W.D. Jackson, W.F. Dickson and Lieutenant N.E. Williams, left at 0314 hours; followed eight minutes later by four more Camels piloted by Captain B.A. Smart, DSC, T.K. Thyne and Lieutenants S. Dawson and W.A. Yeullett. Before these had flown far Thyne was forced to return to *Furious* with a failing engine, but the other six Camels arrived over Tondern as planned. Sweeping in low the first Flight's bombs scored a direct hit on one airship shed; while Smart's second bomb struck the second main shed squarely. Both sheds erupted in flames and billowing smoke, completely destroying two Zeppelins, L 54 and L 60, housed inside. Leaving the objective independently, all six Camel pilots then attempted to return to *Furious* — but only two accomplished this. Yeullett, unable to locate the carrier, was forced down into the sea when his petrol was exhausted and was drowned. Jackson, Williams and Dawson were all obliged to land in neutral Denmark; again, due to lack of fuel. Only Dickson and Smart managed to complete their return journies to the British naval force. Both ditched close to the destroyer *Violent* and were quickly retrieved from their rapidly sinking Camels. It was the first occasion of a land target being successfully raided by carrier-borne aircraft — a great portent for future years of naval air power.

On August 10th, 1918 ships of the Harwich Force set out for the Heligoland Bight area to hunt for German capital ships, and took with it three lighter-borne flying boats and one lighter-borne 2F.1 Camel, N6812, piloted by Lieutenant Stuart Culley; this latter being towed by *HMS Redoubt.* An airborne flying escort, led by the Canadian, Major Robert Leckie, sighted a Zeppelin and accordingly reported this to the main naval task force. Culley was ordered to attempt an interception of the airship and, at 0841 hours, took off successfully from the towed lighter's small wood platform. Climbing steadily with the sun behind him Culley took an hour to get within striking range of the airship, but when still some 200 feet below his target he felt the Camel's controls becoming sluggish as the Camel reached its effective ceiling. N6812 carried two Lewis guns fixed above its upper wing in place of the more usual 2F.1 armament, and Culley had to keep pulling the nose of the Camel up in order to sight his guns. Opening fire at the huge airship above him, Culley had his port Lewis gun jam after firing only a few rounds, but the starboard gun fired a full drum of ammunition. Almost immediately the Zeppelin, L 53, plunged seawards, a roaring furnace of burning gas, and eventually fell into the sea some ten miles south-west of the Borkum Riff light vessel. Only one member of the airship's crew survived the holocaust, by jumping into space at almost three and a half miles above the sea and plummetting into the water — to be rescued shortly after, virtually uninjured! The rest of the crew, including the airship commander Kapitanleutnant Prölss, perished with their ship. With difficulty Culley relocated the British naval force and, with only one pint of fuel remaining in the tank, ditched smoothly alongside his parent destroyer *Redoubt;* the Camel being retrieved intact and returned aboard its lighter. Culley's feat earned him a recommendation for a Victoria Cross, but this was eventually replaced by an actual award of the Distinguished Service Order (DSO).

Typical ship-board 'platform' for a 2.F1, above the main forward gun emplacement housing. Exposed to all weathers, with (usually) merely a rigged canvas 'hangar' at best, and subject to various other stresses of gunfire et al; such Camels provided many problems in pure maintenance.

2.F1 N6779 rigged and stabilised aboard HMS Calliope.

N6779 at Rosyth, having now 'split' into its two body sections for transport back to the ship.

N7103 aboard HMS Royal Sovereign, displaying the damage caused by 15-inch gun fire vibration. This 2.F1 also served aboard HMS Barham; and in October 1918 was based at Rosyth.

Take-off from HMS Pegasus in the Firth of Forth, demonstrating well the very brief take-off length necessary to get any Camel airborne into wind.

Flight Lieutenant Tomlinson leaving HMS Pegasus in N6603. Note the steam 'wind indicator' plume in the bows.

AIRBORNE—another successful take-off from HMS Pegasus.

Numerous experiments were conducted (with a wide variety of aircraft types) in take-off and landing aboard the first flush-decked aircraft carriers in the period 1918-20. First ideas included extensive trials with arrester wires along the deck and appropriate arrester hook gear fixed to aircraft undercarriages; as seen here in the case of a Camel. Three large clips for 'catching' the arrester wires are fixed to the undercarriage spreader bar; while a forward wire guard is for protection of the propeller blades.

2.F1 of 212 Squadron RAF at Great Yarmouth naval air station, 1918, usually piloted by Lt W J Hatcher, MC.

H7343 slung under HMA R23 for 'drop-and-crash' trials of self-sealing fuel tanks in the Camel, at the Hooper works in October 1918.

Apart from its operational successes, the 2F.1 figured in a variety of experiments. Although the rigid airship was foredoomed to a relatively short career, contemporary opinion of such vehicles led to a number of attempts to utilise airships as aircraft carriers. Following earlier, but unsuccessful trials with BE2c aircraft, trials began in July 1918 for use of Camels. Based in a gear devised by members of 212 Squadron RAF**, an aerofoil attachment was fixed under the airship R23 at Pulham Airship Station, to which an F.1, D8250, was affixed by its upper wing, with an additional stay to steady the Camel's rear fuselage. This Camel was taken aloft on November 3rd, 1918 and released; its controls locked and having a dummy in the pilot cockpit. The Camel released smoothly and glided to earth without trouble. Having proved this release gear, a 2F.1, N6814, was similarly attached to R23 at Pulham, and this time the cockpit was occupied by Lieutenant R.E. Keys of 212 Squadron. Dropping away from the airship without incident, Keys then started the Camel's engine, circled round R23, and landed safely at Pulham.

With the war over, further such experiments were temporarily shelved, but as late as February 1921, Camel N7352 figured in an elaborate experiment for testing an overhead-wire 'landing' gear, enabling (it was intended) aircraft to be 'retrieved' by an airship after release — N7352 was fitted with this gear at Grain. Meanwhile, R.E. Keys, DFC, who had joined the RNAS as a rating in 1914 and accumulated 400 flying hours in airships by 1917 when he transferred to aircraft, was involved in several other trials involving 2F.1 Camels during the years 1918-20. Resulting from a suggestion by S.D. Culley, after his L53 experience, one helped to develop an all-steel, jettisonable undercarriage for the Camel; the object being to lighten the aircraft during flight, and to improve safety for seaborne Camel pilots when ditching in the sea after any sortie. On September 20th, 1918 Keys took off from Felixstowe jetty and jettisoned his Camel's undercarriage without mishap. Several other 2F.1's were fitted with such an undercarriage, but the cessation of hostilities with Germany caused the idea to be allowed to lapse. In early 1920 Keys was again prominent in a series of deck-landing and take-off trials from *HMS Eagle* and *Argus* in both 2F.1 Camels and DH9A's. His tragic death on January 10th, 1923 at Stag Lane aerodrome — due to failure of an engine connecting rod during flight — robbed British aviation of yet another true pioneering pilot.

Despite their modest production totals, 2F.1 Camels (unlike their sister F.1's) continued on active service for several years after the 1918 Armistice. At least nine 2F.1's (along with five F.1's) went to Canada at the close of 1918, and of these N7367 was still being flown as late as 1928. A few 2F.1's saw active operational service in the Baltic during anti-Bolshevik operations in 1918-20. Flown from the carrier *Vindictive* and the light cruiser *Delhi,* these Camels occasionally flew from a makeshift aerodrome at Koivisto in 1919. At the beginning of December 1919 at least three 2F.1's (possibly from the *Vindictive* originally) were known to be at Riga with the Latvian forces. All three (and possibly a fourth) survived until at least the summer of 1921; having been flown by the Latvian Aviation Regiment.

Today (1977) there are only two known genuine 2F.1 Camels intact. N8156 was preserved by the National Research Council of Canada; while N6812, the Camel flown by Stuart Culley when he destroyed the L53 on August 10th, 1918, is displayed in the Imperial War Museum in London. If indeed this is Culley's original N6812, it has been subjected to several modifications during its long life; including replacement of Culley's fixed twin-Lewis gun installation by a more standard 2F.1 arrangement of one Vickers and one Lewis. This last was probably first incorporated at Great Yarmouth air station, where N6812 was stationed in October 1918.

**F/n: Known as the Little-Crook Gear, after its patent-holders, Major I.C. Little and Captain E. Crook, RAF.

Splendid view of a 2.F1 Camel (unidentified serial) and its pilot, Major Graham Donald, at Mudros, 1918.

THE SIDE SHOWS

Although in relatively small numbers, Camels played a not insignificant role in several of the so-termed 'side shows' of the war. In the eastern Mediterranean area, where the RNAS virtually monopolised the Allied air effort against Germany's allies Turkey and Bulgaria; RNAS units, with a heterogeneous collection of aircraft types, established a constant threat to enemy troops and shipping. Due to the relatively small numbers of aircraft on actual strength, until 1918 no RNAS unit in this theatre of operations was officially titled with a squadron number; being identified simply alphabetically as 'A', 'B', 'C' Squadrons, RNAS & etc. The first Camel to arrive in the zone went to Mudros, on Lemnos island, on July 26th, 1917, and next day was piloted by Flight Lieutenant John Alcock (of 1919 trans-Atlantic air crossing fame) as one of several RNAS aircraft which attempted to intercept an enemy formation of aircraft approaching Lemnos. Consisting of a large seaplane and two escort scouts, the raiders were engaged by Alcock who managed to send one of the escort machines into the sea. In August more Camels arrived and, on the 10th, three of these moved from Mudros to join B and F Squadrons at Thermi. Only two days later a Camel of D Squadron at Stavros was shot down by enemy fighters.

On September 17th, B Squadron made another move of base, taking its aircraft — which included four Camels by now — from Thermi to Mudros. The RNAS air station at Thermi was transferred to Kalloni (Mitylene) on October 9th; while C Squadron moved to Gliki on Imbros island. Nine days later the few Camels here were fitted with under-fuselage racks and joined a bombing raid on Chanak with favourable results. In general, air combat was spasmodic over the islands of the Aegean, and the relatively few combats which did occur record a high rate of technical defects in the Camels, particularly with gun-jams and ammunition belt feed troubles. Semi-primitive conditions for ground maintenance were unavoidable but accounted for a fairly high unserviceability rate amongst the RNAS units. A big factor was climate which reduced the tempo of any air activity, especially during summer months when most flying was, perforce, restricted to the early morning or late afternoon.

F.1 Camels of 227 Squadron. Nearest two are C133 and C53, both of which were reported at Taranto in late October 1918.

FSL P K Fowler, a New Zealander, with his Camel B6254 of 220 Squadron at Imbros. This Camel also served with 'C' Squadron, RNAS Gliki, and 45 Squadron.

H760, thought to be at Aboukir, Egypt, as a training machine.

C43, an F.1 Camel on the strength of 227 Squadron at Taranto in October 1918.

In January 1918 much of the Allied effort, both air and naval, was concentrated on destruction of two German cruisers, *Goeben* and *Breslau,* whose combined fire-power was a distinct menace to shipping and Allied troop positions. Harassed from the air for almost three weeks continuously, *Breslau* eventually hit a sea mine and sank; but the *Goeben,* despite mine damage, headed for the Dardanelles and then ran aground at Nagara Burnu. On January 20th two Sopwith Baby single-seat floatplanes, each loaded with a single 65lb bomb, attempted to bomb the immobile cruiser, but were attacked over their objective by ten enemy aircraft. The first Baby was almost immediately shot down, but the second, piloted by Flight Sub-Lieutenant Robert Peel, escaped death by the timely arrival of a Camel from the Greek Air Service, piloted by Commander A. Moraitinis, who quickly sent three of Peel's assailants into the sea. Next day eleven DH4's, escorted by Camels, bombed the *Goeben* as the start of a week's continuous air assaults on the marooned ship, before its German crew managed to refloat the cruiser and it escaped to Stenia Bay, Constantinople.

With the formation of the Royal Air Force on April 1st, 1918, air units in the eastern Mediterranean were divided for administrative purposes into two main sections. These were the Aegean Group, comprised of Mudros (Headquarters), and squadrons based at Imbros, Suda Bay, Thasos (which eventually became 222 Squadron), Stavros (where ex-B Squadron, Mitylene became 223 Squadron with two Fighter Flights and a 'mobile' Flight), the base for the Greek Flight, Mitylene, and an airship station at Kassandra. The second section, titled Adriatic Group, comprised an headquarters at Otranto (where six Camels each were allotted to 224 and 225 Squadrons), Taranto (where 226 Squadron was established to have six Camels), and Santa Maria di Leuca, a seaplane base. In May the Aegean Group added a seaplane base at Talikna, and an airfield at Romanos. This re-organisation took several months to finally implement, and the interim air operations continued without undue interruption. In mid-May six DH4's and five Camels were detached from Imbros to Thasos, from where they flew for the next few days on bombing raids against the enemy-held Ruppel Pass, near Drama airfield. The Aegean Group's squadrons concentrated on raiding a host of targets, such as Constantinople, Haida Pasha railway centre, nearby barracks and enemy-occupied docks; the normal formations involved being DH4's escorted by the ubiquitous Camels. Enemy retaliation came on the night of July 5th, when several sneak-raiders bombed Imbros; with one bomb totally destroying one hangar housing seven Camels. Next day six DH4's escorted by the only three serviceable Camels immediately available, bombed an enemy headquarters near the Skumbi river and achieved good results.

Occasional air-to-air combats still occurred, as on July 22nd when Flight Sub-Lieutenants R. Peel and E.P.O. Haughton from Gliki shared in the destruction of a Rumpler two-seater engaged on photo-reconnaissance. In general, however, air combat was mainly a matter of chance encounters at irregular intervals; the Camels' main role being escort for the RAF's bombers. In September 1918 the ex-C Squadron, now at Gliki, was officially retitled to become 220 Squadron, although actual aircraft strength remained — at most — six Camels. In the same month the tide of war forced the Bulgarian forces to start a general retreat which, with the Turks being hard-pressed in Palestine by General Allenby's armies, was the signal for all available Allied air units to start an intensive period of bombing sorties. Some unusual targets were occasionally given to the RAF crews, as on one occasion towards the end of September when a DH4 and two Camels from Imbros were detailed to attack a large train of camels (desert variety . . .) being assembled on the Turkish mainland, south-east of the Straits and about 40 miles inland from Tenedos. Intended as a supply train to reinforce the Turko-German forces in Palestine, these were massacred by the three aircraft whose repeated bombing and strafing completely dissembled the concentration of animals. An outstanding sortie took place on October 2nd, when four formations of two-seat bombers with Camel escorts were assembled at Andrana to raid Durazzo. The first formation — eight DH4's and four Camels — left at 0455 hours and arrived over their objective at 0615 hours. For the following four hours Allied aircraft kept up a continuous assault on Durazzo town, a nearby enemy seaplane base, and several rail sidings. No enemy aircraft opposed the bombers. This raid proved to be the final concentrated air attack of the campaign, and on October 31st, 1918 Turkey obtained an armistice.

Complete line-up of 226 Squadron in August 1918, including Camels D6610, D6614 and C45 identifiable.

Highly decorated but un-identified by serial, this post-Armistice view was taken at Imbros.

THE LAST HURRAH

The morning of November 4th, 1918 dawned mistily over the Western Front in France. Weather 'experts' had forecast that the mist would clear quickly and give way to a bright clear day — conditions which betokened an active day for men of the opposing air services. The weary years of war were nearly done, and already rumours were rife of a request from Germany for a ceasefire, an armistice, as a prelude to possible peace talks. To the Camel pilots of 65 Squadron at Bisseghem airfield, however, it was simply another day of 'business as usual'. Orders had been received the previous evening for an Offensive Patrol to be mounted in the early morning, and accordingly, just before 0900 hours, nine of 65's Camels were airborne and climbing towards the fighting zone to seek out German aircraft. Within minutes they linked up with eight more Camels from 204 Squadron, from the ex-German airfield at Heule, and together the two formations continued to climb to a patrol height of 12,000 feet over the area south-east of Ghent.

Leading the 65 Squadron element was a veteran Camel 'ace' Captain John L.M. White, whose deputy was another experienced pilot Captain Maurice Newnham, already credited with 15 victories. Spearheading the rear 204 Squadron formation was yet another Camel veteran, Captain C.P. Allen. As the Camels flew above Zonneghem, John White spotted two large formations of German fighters heading towards him from the east, and soon identified them as Fokker D VII's — high quality opposition. The larger of the German batches numbered about 40 Fokkers, while the other formation comprised perhaps two dozen of the straight-winged D.VII's. Collectively these presented a formidable, if colourful array; the bigger formation having light blue fuselages with tail assemblies chequered in yellow and green, and the smaller gaggle sporting red-painted noses and pure white tails. The odds against the Camels were almost four-to-one.

White gave one last swift glance around the upper sky for any other German aircraft, looked left and right at the Camel formation, then raised his gloved hand and led his men down under the the larger of the two Fokker formations. Within seconds all semblance of formation was dissembled as the sky became a maelstrom of twisting, turning aircraft; the confused mass of opposing fighters breaking up into a myriad of individual duels as each pilot sought the deadly tail position of his enemy. One D VII curved in behind White who quickly exploited the Camel's legendary turning ability and immediately reversed the positions. Firing a long burst from only 20 feet range, White saw the Fokker flick onto its back, and then watched as both of the Fokker's mainplanes fell away from its fuselage and its tail assembly disintegrated. Only seconds later another D VII bore in behind White's Camel. Kicking the Camel into two fast spin-turns, White came out in a curving right-hand turn to fasten on this German's tail. The Fokker pilot promptly climbed for vital height but White's fire hit him quickly and the D VII fell away pouring white smoke until it reached 2,000 feet, where it exploded in a gout of flames. Pausing briefly to take in the general situation, White noticed one German spraying bullets in 'hose-fashion' at any Camel within range, and therefore nosed down to engage it. The two fighters approached each other head-on, both pilots firing steadily. White's tracers hit the Fokker's nose, causing the German to stop firing and zoom over the Camel's top wing, hesitate, and then spin down erupting flames. Seeing a lone D VIII below him,

*65 Squadron group, including (from left)
Captain A G Jones-Williams; Captain Maurice
Newnham; Major H V Champion de Crespigny,
DSO, MC (OC Sqn); Unknown; Captain A
Storey, DFC.*

White dived on its tail and fired several crisp bursts. The Fokker spun down to 6,000 feet and then broke fast eastwards in a bid to escape, but White had followed him down and immediately re-opened fire. Again the German pilot went into a fast spin but was eventually lost to sight in the ground haze.

Five thousand feet above John White, two Fokkers were giving their undivided attentions to White's deputy, Maurice Newnham. Shaking off one D VII, Newnham got behind the other and slammed in a burst from only 10 yards range. The Fokker jerked sideways and began to spin, then reared in a stall, and fell away in a vertical spin from which it never recovered. Its markings seemed to Newnham to suggest its pilot was a formation leader. Attacking a second Fokker, Newnham fired a series of brief bursts at pointblank range. This D VII climbed wildly, its pilot clearly dead and slumped forward in his cockpit, and on reaching the stall point fell into a vertical dive and plunged straight down into the earth.

By now the general melee had spread itself all over the sky, at levels varying between 14,000 and 4,000 feet. Lieutenant W.R. Allison of 65 Squadron claimed two victories — the first being shot off a Camel's tail with a burst of 10 yards range which caused the Fokker to burst into flames. His second victim was also already engaged with a Camel before Allison poured in 100 rounds from 50 yards range and sent it down to crash. An American attached to 65 Squadron. Lieutenant F.R. Pemberton, USAS, was wounded early in the first clash, but stayed in the fight and attacked a Fokker at 12,000 feet from head-on. When only 20 yards apart, the D VII fell into a tight spin and then tore itself apart in an obscene tangle of wreckage. Nearby Pemberton's close friend Second Lieutenant A.J. Cleare dived on a Fokker engaged with a Camel, and at 25 yards saw his own bullets enter the back of the German pilot, who fell forward in his seat. The Fokker rolled onto its back and fell in a series of crazy curves until it reached 5,000 feet, when it dived straight into the ground at full power and exploded.

Elsewhere in the sprawling mass dogfight individual combats raged on for perhaps two minutes — then, with eerie suddenness peculiar to all air fighting, the sky seemed to empty of aircraft. After returning to their airfields the Camel pilots compared notes and totted up their claims and losses. 65 Squadron's pilots put in justifiable claims for totals of ten enemy aircraft destroyed and a further seven out of control or decisively driven down. 204 Squadron's share in the destruction amounted to two destroyed and five out of control. Camel losses amounted to three pilots 'Missing' (one of whom was later reported as a prisoner of war) and Pemberton wounded. A possible total of 27 pilots killed or 'Missing' in the brief space of less than 30 minutes of furious fighting. . .

It was one of the last mass dogfights of the 1914-18 war, although fighting — and losses — continued right up until the cease-fire was promulgated on November 11th. As such it not only exemplified a form of air combat not uncommon during the closing months of the war, but demonstrated the deadly ability of the Camel when flown by experienced men. By that time the Sopwith Camel's design was two years old — virtually a lifetime in terms of wartime aircraft — and its operational career had lasted eighteen months; yet it had remained the supreme dogfighter of its era. Against machines superior in sheer speed and climbing ability, the Camel's unrivalled manoeuvrability gave it an unchallenged supremacy when met in its own element. It was indeed the King of combat. . .

F1946 converted to dual cockpit at the Australian training camp, Minchinhampton in 1918.

An unidentified dual-seat conversion in use at 204 TDS, Eastchurch; bearing the numerals '13' under each wing, and possibly B5713 which was known to be there in this guise.

Variation in tandem cockpits was B5575 at Shotwick (later re-named RAF Sealand) in mid-1918. In cockpit is an American pilot, Lt L MacLean Lord, USAS. Inscription alongside the cockpit read, 'Not to be flown without Passenger'.

Sopwith Scooter in July 1918 at Brooklands.

Air-testing the Scooter at Brooklands.

Recorded on the Civil Air Register as G-EACZ, the Scooter was finally scrapped in 1927.

Second of Sopwith's single-seat monoplane projects was the Swallow, B9276, seen here at Brooklands in October 1918, fitted with a 110hp Clerget rotary engine and twin Vickers guns.

Sopwith Swallow and Scooter

Sopwith's first venture in monoplane configuration was the Sopwith Monoplane No. 1, which later became titled Scooter. By fitting a standard (un-serialled) F.1 Camel fuselage with a single, parasol wing, RAF wire-braced from a single cabane above the centre-section; the firm's first single-wing machine was first flown in June 1918, and then become virtually a 'runabout' machine for use by Sopwith's chief test pilot, Harry Hawker. At the end of the war the Scooter was temporarily registered as K-135 to the parent company, and in mid-1919 was re-registered as G-EACZ. In April 1921 Harry Hawker purchased the Scooter for private use, but after his death three months later the machine was placed in storage until 1925. Completely overhauled on behalf of a Mr. C. Clayton of Hendon, the Scooter received its Certificate of Airworthiness on August 1st, 1925. In the following year the Scooter changed ownership again, being bought by Dudley Watt, and subsequently entered for a number of aerial sporting events; the last being at Lympne on September 18th, 1926. In 1927 the Sopwith Scooter was scrapped.

Sopwith Monoplane No. 2, later titled Swallow, was officially contracted to be built on the authority of the Air Board, and its general design owed much to the Scooter. Utilising the fuselage of F.1 Camel B9276, the Swallow differed in two main particulars from its predecessor. Its wings were of greater span, with longer ailerons and a distinct six-degrees' sweep-back from the front centre point. Additionally, it was armed with twin Vickers machine guns, set slightly further apart than on a standard F.1 Camel, and without the Camel's hump fairing housing for the guns' breeches. Intended as a fighter, possibly for use with the Fleet, the Swallow passed its acceptance tests at Brooklands in October 1918, and was then flown by Harry Hawker to Martlesham Heath for Service trials on October 30th. A series of minor faults and fuel supply problems prolonged the official test programme until May 1919, after which the machine was scrapped.

TF.1 Trench Fighter

As a direct result of the experience gained in 1917 by Camels (and other types of single-seaters) used in low-level ground attack roles, and particularly in deference to the high loss rate amongst such aircraft; an armoured trench-strafing development of the F.1 Camel appeared in February 1918, designated TF.1 ('Trench Fighter.1'). Powered by a 110hp Le Rhone, the TF.1 was a direct modification of F.1 B9278. In place of the standard twin Vickers guns' installation, two Lewis guns were fixed to fire at an angle downwards and forward, through the flooring of the cockpit; while a third Lewis was mounted above the upper wing centre-section in similar fashion to the 2F.1 Ships Camel. The underside of the forward fuselage was armoured from the engine compartment to the rear of the cockpit.

First flown at Brooklands on February 15th, 1918, the TF.1 was sent to France on March 7th and returned to Brooklands a week later. In general performance the TF.1 was inferior to standard production F.1 Camels, and the concept of downward-firing armament for ground attack roles was already proven as less effective than a fighter's normal gun arrangement. Possibly a more cogent reason for discarding the TF.1 — it was dismantled by Sopwith on its return from France — was the existence of the Sopwith Salamander, designed specifically for the trench-strafing tactic; the prototype of which underwent Service appraisal in France in May 1918.

Above and Left: Two views of the Sopwith TF.1 'Trench Fighter', B9278, both taken on February 19th, 1918. Both views show clearly the twin stripped Lewis guns' installation firing downwards.

A 'MYSTERY' CAMEL! Fitted with a 160hp Gnome Monosoupape rotary engine, and (apparently) wearing USAS roundels under its lower wings; there is also clearly a Holt Flare fitted below the starboard lower wing. The 'mystery' extension-cum-fitment through the propeller boss might possibly be the Gnome Engine Company's grapeshot gun (French Patent No. 504. 255) though no authentic confirmation has yet been unearthed to substantiate this theory.

134

Captain S M Kinkead, DSO, DSC, DFC and his Camel of 'B' Flight, 47 Squadron in Russia, 1919. The fuselage roundel appears to be coloured white, blue, red (from centre).

POST–ARMISTICE

Although the major European conflict officially halted on November 11th, 1918, this armistice was merely a signal for the upsurge of several minor wars and revolutions in various European and Baltic countries. The largest of these, in terms of people involved and area, concerned the continuing struggle between supporters of the defunct Czarist regime in Russia and the 'Red' revolutionary Bolshevik movement which had overthrown centuries of autocratic imperial rule in the massive and bloody uprising of 1917. The British Government offered substantial aid to the 'White Russian' cause — the anti-Bolshevik movement — and the start of Britain's commitment to a Russian 'campaign' can be traced to the peace treaty signed between Russia and Germany in March 1918. Of immediate concern then was the Allies' need to prevent German establishment of submarine bases in the Arctic ports of Archangel and Murmansk, and the denial of resources in western Siberia to Germany and the Central powers. Consequently Britain organised the North Russia Expeditionary Force; the first elements of which landed at Murmansk in June 1918. In the following month the seaplane carrier Nairana arrived with a complement of eight aircraft, one of which was a Camel which participated in several operational sorties during the next months. These operations led to the occupation of Archangel and other vital ports, and in October 1918 the Nairana returned to England.

F5234, the private property of an American, K M Murray, a member of the 7th Kosciuszko Fighter Squadron, Polish Air Service, and emblazoned with this unit's badge. It reached the unit, from USA, in July 1920.

In India's sunny clime— F1915 at Risalpur, North West Frontier Province of India (now titled Pakistan) in 1919. Probably one of 31 Squadron's motley collection of various aircraft types.

F.1 in USA markings, fitted with 150hp Monosoupape engine, at Martlesham Heath in October 1917.

On November 12th, 1918 six Camels were despatched to this Expeditionary Force, and in December the RAF element in North Russia was re-organised into two separate commands; one at Archangel and the other at Murmansk. Further RAF units — mainly two-seat aircraft squadrons — were sent, or formed, in the Aegean zone and along the shores of the Black Sea; including 221 Squadron which had at least one Camel on strength, flown normally by Major J.O. Andrews, DSO, MC. In April 1919 an RAF 'Training Mission' left England bound for Novorossik in South Russia and arrived in May, being then reinforced by 47 Squadron from Salonika. A composite unit, 47 Squadron's equipment included a Flight ('B') of Sopwith Camels. In North Russia a number of Camels were among the aircraft equipping the Slavo-British Group, the leading fighter pilot of this formation being Major Alexander Kazakov, the top-scoring Russian 'ace' of 1914-18. News of an international withdrawal of the British from North Russia was received by the Group on July 28th, 1919, and Kazakov became noticeably morose and withdrawn. On the evening of August 3rd, the day on which the British air element proposed to hold a farewell dinner for their Russian friends, Kazakov appeared at the hangars and ordered his Camel to be made ready. Taking off in an obviously angry mood, he kept the Camel at a mere 20 feet height for a short distance, then pulled the machine up sharply as if to loop. The Camel fell off the top of its arc, stalled, and plunged vertically into the centre of the aerodrome. Kazakov, Russian 'Ace of aces', died cradled in the arms of the noted British pilot, Ira Jones.

In South Russia 47 Squadron's few Camels gave sterling service in difficult circumstances and conditions. From June 13th, 1919 the squadron was commanded by the Canadian Camel 'ace' Ray Collishaw, DSO, DSC, DFC until he was succeeded in command by Major G.R.M. Reid in April 1920; but the unit was normally led in action by another ex-RNAS Camel veteran, Captain S.M. Kinkead, DSO, DSC, DFC. Much of the Camels' duties was in the ground-attack role, but at least 20 air-to-air victories were claimed by Camel pilots from 47 Squadron. Air opposition to the Camels was a motley mixture of ex-wartime machines, including Nieuports, Fokker Triplanes, Albatros, Pfalz, Spads, and even Sopwith 1½ Strutters. Although available records for the campaign are scanty, 47's first air victory would appear to have been credited to Captain M.H. Aten, the squadron adjutant, in April 1919 when he shot down one of a pair of Nieuport scouts; his victim crashing on the bank of the Volga river. The highest-scoring individual Camel pilot was undoubtedly 'Sam' Kinkead, who accounted for at least eight, and possibly ten Russian aircraft in air combats. In one fight during May. Kinkead was shot down by a Fokker Triplane and force-landed in enemy territory. His companion, Captain R.H. Daly, DSC, an ex-210 Squadron veteran, immediately landed alongside Kinkead's crash, and Kinkead squeezed himself under the Camel's centre-section on top of the guns' hump, in which precarious position he was flown to safety. Lack of positive evidence precludes details of every combat in which the Camels participated, but it is known, for example, that Kinkead shot down a Nieuport on October 30th, 1919 while flying Camel F1955. Other squadron pilots known to have achieved victories were Captain M.H. Aten (5), R.H. Daly (3) — whose Camel had red-painted wing tips, and W Burns-Thompson (2). This latter pilot was later killed in Camel F6302 when carrying out low-level stunting over the RAF station at Abu Sueir, Egypt on November 4th, 1922. Ray Collishaw who occasionally flew Camel F6396 added an Albatros scout destroyed and another out of control to his impressive war tally of 60 victories. In October 1919, 47 Squadron was retitled to become 'A' Squadron, RAF Training Mission, South Russia and remained on operations until April 1920 when, along with other RAF units, it was finally withdrawn from Russia. The faithful Camels were given an ignominious fate by being lined up to Novorossik harbour and then crushed to rubble by an army tank. The tank next crushed 40 new, crated DH9's, and met its own demise by being driven straight into the harbour water and 'drowned'.

Camel 2F.1, N6616 in Estonian markings at Koivisto, Lithuania in 1919-20 during anti-Bolshevik operations.

Latvian 2F.1's at Riga on August 7th, 1921.

Latvian 2F.1 Camel (ex-N8187) in flight over Riga.

138

POLAND

Another struggle for independence in which Camels were involved was the post-1918 Russo-Polish war. Towards the end of 1919 the Polish Air Force decided to acquire a number of British aircraft for its combat units, and the official purchases, which included 105 Bristol F2b's, were supplemented by a gift to the Polish Government by King George V of 12 DH9's and 20 single-seat fighters. The 'presentation' fighters comprised ten Sopwith Dolphins, one Martinsyde F4, three or four SE5A's and either five or six Sopwith Camels — precise totals of SE's and Camels are not documented. These finally reached Polish air units in August 1920, having been originally promised for delivery in March 1920 but delayed by a strike by British dockers refusing to handle 'war' material' to Poland. At the beginning of August the 19th Fighter Squadron was equipped with all ten Dolphins, but these were only used operationally for about six weeks and were then replaced by Spad 13's. There appears to be no positive evidence that the few Camels were ever issued to first-line Polish combat units, though several unconfirmed accounts credit the 7th *Kosciuszko* Fighter Squadron with receiving and operating Camels. Such accounts possibly refer to the one known operational Camel, F5234; the private property of an American citizen Kenneth M. Murray, which was indeed brought on the strength of the *Koscuisako* squadron at Lwow and used on active service from July 1920. It seems much more likely that the 'gift' Camels were used only for training purposes. At least one Polish Camel survived until 1922 at Lwow, where General L. Rayski, during a routine inspection tour of his air units, expressed a wish to fly the solitary Camel. On take-off, however, its engine failed and Rayski crashed badly, injuring his face.

U.S.A.

Despite the fact that a known total of 325 Camels were eventually transferred or sent to the United States Air Services during 1918-19 — one purchase in June 1918 for 143 Camels was to supply the American Camel squadrons in France — relatively few actually found their way to the American homeland. This is not surprising when the normal Service attrition rate on operations is taken into account; an example of which being the 17th Aero Squadron, USAS which received a total of 66 aircraft and 'consumed' (sic) 47 of these in a mere sixteen weeks of active service. One of the earliest Camels to undergo American trials was F1515, which was exhaustively tested by Lieutenant Roth at the US Experimental Field at Choisy-le-Roi during the first week of September 1918. At the end of the war at least two Camels existed in the USA, in use by the US Navy; one being aboard *USS Arkansas,* and the other with *USS Texas.* It was the latter Camel which was flown by LCDR E.O. McDonnell on March 9th, 1919 to make the first-ever flight from a turret platform on an American battleship, when he took off from the No. 2 gun turret of *USS Texas* as it lay at anchor at Guantanamo.

The general air-mindedness of the US Navy at that period is reflected in its request in early 1919 for 150 aircraft to be allotted for use with the Fleet. A further request to the US Army in July 1919 was for 16 Camels — eight to go to Hampton Roads and San Diego naval bases — 'or Nieuport 28's' (sic), plus 16 Sopwith 1½ Strutters; these totals being considered a 'fair proportion' of the 74 Camels (and other aircraft) reported in April 1919 by the Director of the Air Services as being returned from Europe to the USA. In the same month another US Army report gave the disposition of Camels *actually* in the USA as; three in crates at Wilbur Wright Field, Ohio; three at Langley Field, Virginia; and a '. . . large number of Sopwith Camels, 1½ Strutters, and Nieuport 28's. . .' scattered at various other US Army fields. At McCook Field were reported to be one Sopwith Salamander and one Sopwith Dolphin. Contemporary US Service documents are by no means specific when relating to Camels, often using the generic title 'Sopwiths', which could equally have applied to other Sopwith designs.

F.1 Camel, F6302, photo-graphed at Abu Sueir, Egypt, late 1922. It was wrecked on November 4th, 1922, killing its pilot, and the remains of the aircraft were simply 'buried' in the sand. Entered on the British Civil Register as G-EBER, it was never actually pain-ted with this registration.

F6394, fitted with an en-larged rudder and a 180hp Le Rhone 9R rotary en-gine. Seen at Martlesham Heath in February 1919.

F.1, H2700 which first flew on December 12th, 1919, and was allotted the civil registration G-EAWN in March 1921. Seen here participating in the Aerial Derby on July 16th, 1921.

140

On July 3rd, 1919 a total of 28 cases of 'Sopwiths' were unshipped at New York and despatched to the Aviation General Supply Depot at Americus, Georgia; following which the US Army authorities agreed to supply the requested naval allocation for Fleet service. In order to prepare any intended naval aircraft with flotation gear and hydrovanes, the US Naval Station at Hampton Roads was designated as the base for all battleship scouts, where all such machines were to be assembled, modified and tested prior to re-issue to specific naval units. Seven Camels and 13 1½ Strutters were initially allocated in July 1919 for possible use on the *USS Pennsylvania, Arizona, Oklahoma* and *Nevada;* while *USS Texas* transferred two Camels to Hampton Broads, via Langley Field, for modification; and two other Camels were transferred from the Army to the naval base on September 21st, 1919. On September 1st, 1919 an order was sent to the Naval Aircraft Factory at Philadelphia to give top priority to the supply of 28 aircraft, of varying types, complete with guns, ammunition and flotation gear, for Atlantic and Pacific Fleet detachments by January 1st, 1920. Of this total at least six were Camels, which were allotted American serials A5658, A5659, A5721, A5722, A5723 and A5724. Two other Camels received at this time at San Diego base were serialled A5759 and A5730. A5721 was despatched to the NAF, Philadelphia from Hampton Roads on September 29th, 1919; while three others (identities unknown) arrived in November.

The US Navy's hopes for an adequate air arm were abruptly shattered on November 17th, 1919. On that date the Director of the Air Service (Army) reported that only four Camels had been actually delivered to the Navy, and that there were '. . . only six Camels left in the whole of the Air Service . . .' His report concluded by stating emphatically that it was, '. . . impossible to make any further transfers to the Navy.' The six Camels referred to as being the US Army's 'sole Camels' included four which had left Bordeaux, France on September 2nd, 1919, bound for New York, and which had been already earmarked to go to Kelly Field for training purposes. In spite of this blow, the Philadelphia Naval Aviation Factory completed its immediate commitment to test future naval scouts. One test of flotation gear on December 3rd, 1919 was flown by First Lieutenant G.B. Newman, USMC from Bustleton Field. After climbing his Camel to 3,000 feet, he descended to 1,500 feet over a nearby river, jettisoned the wheeled undercarriage, and prepared to ditch in the river. Opening the air bottles intended to inflate the two under-wing flotation air bags, Newman set the Camel down smoothly and 'landed' tail-first. The aircraft tipped to 40 degrees and sank quickly nose-first. After Newman and the Camel had been retrieved it was discovered that the air bags were still folded in their stowage position — no reason for their non-inflation being elicited.

As in most countries, the Camel found little application in civil guise in the USA. A former F.1, C28, came on to the US Civil Register as Nc3938, and a second Camel — original serial unidentified — is believed to have been registered in January 1929. At least one genuine Camel survived to be included in the famous collection of 1914-18 aircraft owned by Colonel G.B. Jarrett in the 1920's. This particular Camel was later drastically refurbished by Frank Tallman, and became one of the 'Tallmantz' collection of flying veterans. Its given serial N6254 bore no relation to any Camel production batch; N6254 being originally allotted to one of a batch of Spad S7's ordered from the Mann Egerton firm of Norwich, Norfolk which was eventually cancelled. An original manufacturer's name plate of the British Caudron Company of London was fixed to this Camel, but several departures from original Camel construction lay-out were necessary to conform with modern flight safety regulations, and to fabricate assemblies no longer available in original states. In more recent years a number of other 'Camels' have been built by devotees of 1914-18 aviation history — perhaps not entirely authentic in every detail, but sufficiently so to perpetuate the 'feel' and unmistakeable profile of Sopwith's 'fierce little beast' . . .

N8156, a 2F.1 at Camp Borden, Canada in
the summer of 1928.

The 45hp Anzani-engined F.1 Camel owned
by Grenville Manton at one period. Many
years later the basic aircraft was finally completely refurbished and is now held by the
Royal Air Force Museum at Hendon, near
London.

UNITED KINGDOM

Unlike its more tractable stable companion, the delightful Pup, the fiery Camel found little use in the British postwar scene. By January 1920 the few remaining Camel units of the RAF had either exchanged their aircraft for the more powerful Snipes, or had been reduced to cadre and disbanded. Just two F.1 Camels came on to the British Civil Register. The first of these, H2700, owned by Captain Hubert Broad, became G-EAWN in March 1921, and was flown to sixth placing in that year's Aerial Derby. It was dismantled at Stag Lane aerodrome in the following year. The second civil Camel, F6302, also had a brief career. Registered as G-EBER — though these codings were never applied to the aircraft — it had served with 226 Squadron RAF in late 1918, and was bought as government surplus at RAF Abu Sueir, Egypt in mid-1922 by Flying Officer E.J. McDonough, to whom it was registered. On November 4th that same year Flying Officer W Burns-Thompson took the Camel up for a local 'flip'. Sweeping low over a soccer match being played at the RAF station, he started a series of stunt manoeuvres, but hit the hospital roof and crashed on the officers' Mess, being killed on impact. No attempt was made to reconstruct the Camel which, complete with spare engine still crated, was 'buried' on the airfield.

At the Royal Aircraft Establishment, Farnborough a number of Camels continued for several years after 1918 as vehicles for a variety of experimental trials. In February 1920, B2312 and H7363 were fitted with Imber self-sealing fuel tanks for tests; while D1965 and F6456 were used for prolonged testing in the context of inverted spinning trials, in the experienced hands of such pilots as Squadron Leader Roderic Hill, Flight Lieutenant E.R.C. Scholefield, and Flying Officer H.A. Hamersley. For inverted flying trials F6456 was fitted with additional flying wires in the centre bay in 1923.

The only F.1 Camel to survive to the present day in the United Kingdom now resides in the Royal Air Force Museum at Hendon, north of London. The history of this particular F.1 is still far from completely recorded, despite many years of research by various people directly concerned. From authentic AID stamps and marks on the original airframe it would appear to have been first built in July 1918 by the Norwich firm of Boulton & Paul, yet its original serial number is still unconfirmed. In the early 1920's it was purchased from the Aircraft Disposal Company at Waddon — less engine — by its first private owner Grenville Manton, who converted the airframe to receive a 45 hp six-cylinder Anzani radial engine. When flown by Manton in this state, he found the rudder area inadequate and the whole aircraft woefully under-powered. Manton then sold the Camel to,' . . . an enthusiast who towed it by a small Fiat car from Tring, Hertfordshire to his home in North Wales.' Its subsequent career is fragmentary until it was discovered, in poor condition, in Essex and acquired by R.G.J. Nash for his pre-1939 collection of vintage aircraft. In the interim the Camel had been marked with spurious Lafayette Escadrille fuselage insignia, and the remnants of its serial number eluded positive identification; only the last three digits — '508' — of a four-digit number being identifiable. Accordingly — though with what reasoning is not known — the Camel was re-serialled as H508, and appeared at several public displays and functions in this guise, after careful restoration to its (presumed) Clerget-engined condition.

In more recent years a team of enthusiasts made a deep investigation into this Camel's true identity, but failed to establish this with absolute certainty. Carefully restoring the aircraft, the team applied fuselage markings of 43 Squadron RFC/RAF and the serial F6314 — the reasoning for which is unknown to the author. Purchased by the Royal Aeronautical Society in the 1950's the Camel was eventually re-marked with its present 65 Squadron unit markings, but retained the serial F6314, and placed on permanent display in the aircraft gallery of the Royal Air Force Museum at Hendon, where it may be seen today.

APPENDICES 1—13

1. Production batches & manufacturers

2. Rebuilt Camels

3. Dimensions, weights, performances

4. Rigging notes & diagrams

5. Main variations

6. Service use (units)

7. Camel squadrons, November 11th, 1918

8. Victory claims

9. Notes for student pilots

10. Ditching

11. Parachute harness

12. Example serials by squadron/unit

13. Presentation Camels

Appendix 1

PRODUCTION BATCHES

A total of 5,597 F.1 and 317 2F.1's were ordered, and almost all were built and/or delivered to the Services. As indicated in the tables below, of this overall total of 5,914 Camels, of all types, ordered; 140 F.1's remain unconfirmed as actually built or delivered, while twenty 2F.1's were definitely not built, and a further twenty 2F.1's are unconfirmed as either built or delivered. For the sake of clarity, Camel contracts eventually cancelled are not included here; while rebuilt Camels, contracted or uncontracted, are listed separately in Appendix 2.

Sopwith F.1

N517 & N518	Prototypes	2
B2301 — B2550	Ruston, Proctor	250
B3751 — B3950	Sopwith	200
B4601 — B4650	Portholme Aerodrome	50
B5151 — B5250	Boulton & Paul	100
B5401 — B5450	Hooper	50
B5551 — B5650	Ruston, Proctor	100
B5651 — B5750	Clayton & Shuttleworth	100
B6201 — B6450	Sopwith	250
B7131 — B7180	Portholme Aerodrome	50
B7181 — B7280	Clayton & Shuttleworth	100
B7281 — B7480	Ruston, Proctor	200
B9131 — B9330	Boulton & Paul	200
C1 — C200	Nieuport & General	200
C1551 — C1600	Hooper	50
C1601 — C1700	Boulton & Paul	100
C3281 — C3380	Boulton & Paul	100
C6701 — C6800	British Caudron	100
C8201 — C8300	Ruston, Proctor	100
C8301 — C8400	March, Jones & Cribb	100
D1776 — D1975	Ruston, Proctor	200
D3326 — D3425	Clayton & Shuttleworth	100
D6401 — D6700	Boulton & Paul	300
D8101 — D8250	Ruston, Proctor	150
D9381 — D9530	Boulton & Paul	150
D9531 — D9580	Portholme Aerodrome	50
D9581 — D9680	Clayton & Shuttleworth	100
E1401 — E1600	Ruston, Proctor	200
E4374 — E4423	Clayton & Shuttleworth	50
E5129 — E5178	Portholme Aerodrome	50
E7137 — E7336	Ruston, Proctor	200
F1301 — F1550	Boulton & Paul	250
F1883 — F1957	Boulton & Paul	75
F1958 — F2007	Portholme Aerodrome	50
F2008 — F2082	Ruston, Proctor	75
F2083 — F2182	Hooper	100
F3096 — F3145	Clayton & Shuttleworth	50
F3196 — F3245	Nieuport & General	50
F3918 — F3967	Nieuport & General	50
F3968 — F4067	Ruston, Proctor	100
F4974 — F5073	Clayton & Shuttleworth	100 (a)
F5174 — F5248	March, Jones & Cribb	75
F6301 — F6500	Boulton & Paul	200
F8496 — F8595	Nieuport & General	100
F8646 — F8695	Portholme Aerodrome	50 (b)
H734 — H833	Hooper	100 (c)
H2646 — H2745	Boulton & Paul	100 (d)
H7343 — H7412	Hooper	70 (e)
N6330 — N6379	Sopwith	50 (f)

Sopwith 2F.1 'Ships Camel'

N4 & N5	Prototypes	2
N6600 — N6649	Sopwith	50
N6750 — N6849	William Beardmore	100 (g)
N7100 — N7149	William Beardmore	50
N7350 — N7389	Arrol, Johnston	40 (h)
N8130 — N8179	Hooper	50 (i)
N8180 — N8204	Clayton & Shuttleworth	25

Manufacturers (Registered Offices)

Arrol, Johnston Ltd, Dumfries, Scotland
Boulton & Paul Ltd, Rose Lane, Norwich, Norfolk
British Caudron Ltd, Broadway, Cricklewood, London
Clayton & Shuttleworth Ltd, Lincoln
Hooper & Co Ltd, St James's Street, London
March, Jones & Cribb Ltd, Leeds
Nieuport & General Aircraft Ltd, Langton Rd
 Cricklewood, London
Portholme Aerodrome Ltd, St John's St, Huntingdon
Ruston, Proctor & Co Ltd, Lincoln
Sopwith Aviation Co Ltd, Canbury Park Rd,
 Kingston-upon-Thames, Surrey
William Beardmore & Co Ltd, Dalmuir, Glasgow,
 Scotland
No. 3 Aircraft Repair Depot, Yate, Bristol
 (Rebuild Contracts)

(a)	— Only up to F5025 inc known as built
(b)	— Only up to F8673 inc known as built
(c)	— Only up to H833 confirmed as built/delivered
(d)	— Only up to H2724 confirmed as delivered
(e)	— Only up to H7363 confirmed as built/delivered
(f)	— N6338 re-serialled B3977, retained by Sopwith, later transferred to RFC.
(g)	— Last ten sub-contracted to Arrol, Johnston
(h)	— Only 20 built/delivered
(i)	— Only to N8159 confirmed as built/delivered

KNOWN REBUILT CAMELS

With the daily attrition of aircraft, the bulk of which occurred in flying accidents of one sort or another, reclamation of repairable airframes became almost a major 'industry' within the RFC and RAF. Rebuilt aircraft were almost invariably allotted 'new' serial numbers in order to avoid ambiguity in Quartermasters' returns and records. Thus a large number of Camels were re-used operationally with serial identities which do not tie in with contracted production batches — a fact which has created no little confusion in the past amongst aviation archivists and historians. Due to the unrelated circumstances in which such rebuilds were produced it is impossible to present any truly comprehensive listing of these Camels. However, the list below are rebuilt Camels positively confirmed as being built and issued to the Services; a total of 387 Camels. It must be emphasised that many others may well have existed; evidence of which would be welcomed by this author.

CONTRACTED REBUILDS (SALVAGE)

E9964 — E9983	No 3 ARD, Yate	20
F2189 — F2208	No 3 ARD, Yate	20
F4177 — F4216	No 3 ARD, Yate	40

UNCONTRACTED REBUILDS

B778	— 1 ARD, Farnborough; 4 AFC Sqn & shot down 4/9/18
B900	— 73 Sqn & crashed 17/3/18
B3296	— 'HAPPY HAWKINS'; Isle of Wight, Oct 1918
B3312	— 3 (N) Sqn
B3328	— 209 Sqn
B3338	— 209 Sqn
B3353	— 3 (N) Sqn
B3371	— 3 (N) Sqn
B3376	— 203 Sqn (Capt E T Hayne, 5 victories)
B3383	— 'CITY OF HULL, AUSTRALIA'
B3992	— 209 Sqn
B3998	— 209 Sqn
B7125	— 203 Sqn
B7743	— 1 ARD
B7744	— 65 Sqn
B7745	— 1 ARD; converted two-seater, Joyce Green, 1918
B7746	— 1 ARD
B7756	— 1 ARD
B7790	— UK Training Sqn
B7791	— Joyce Green, 1918
B7804	— 65 Sqn & lost 28/9/18
B7820	— Joyce Green, 1918
B7821	— Joyce Green, 1918
B7859	— 65 Sqn
B7860	— 1 ARD; 204 Sqn; 210 Sqn
B7864	— 65 Sqn
B7867	— 73 Sqn
B7868	— 73 Sqn & lost 8/8/18
B7869	— 1 ARD; 148th Aero Sqn, USAS
B7874	— 73 Sqn & lost 25/7/18
B7883	— 70 Sqn
B7896	— 1 ARD; 17th Aero Sqn, USAS
B7905	— 1 ARD; 3 Sqn RFC
B7932	— 73 Sqn, Jan 1918
B7968	— 1 (N) Sqn, June 1917
B8025	— 1 ARD
B8155	— 1 ARD; 148th Aero Sqn, USAS
B8187	— 204 Sqn
B8830	— 6th Wing, Dover
B8921	— Joyce Green, 1918
D1599	— 150 Sqn (Lt D. A. Davies, 8 victories)
D9153	— 46 Sqn (9-victories aircraft)

E7235	— 73 Sqn
E7292	— 73 Sqn
E7302	— 73 Sqn
E9964	— E9983 inc — Built at 3 ARD
F2189	— F2208 inc — Built at 3 ARD
F2328	— 210 Sqn (Lt C.F. Pineau, 5 victories)
F4175	— Built locally by 112 (HD) Sqn
F4177	— F4216 inc — built by 3 ARD
F913	— 213 Sqn
F5914	— 201 Sqn; 210 Sqn, 'S' & lost 22/7/18
F5918	— 201 Sqn
F5919	— France
F5920	— 73 Sqn & lost 18/7/18
F5921	— 80 Sqn & lost 2/10/18
F5925	— 209 Sqn
F5926	— 54 Sqn & lost 2/10/18
F5927	— 80 Sqn
F5930	— 210 Sqn
F5932	— 73 Sqn, Jan 1918
F5938	— 3 Sqn RFC
F5939	— 201 Sqn
F5941	— 'E' of A Flt, 201 Sqn. 1918
F5942	— 'Z' of 65 Sqn
F5943	— 148th Aero Sqn, USAS
F5944	— 209 Sqn
F5945	— 73 Sqn, crashed 4/9/18; 148th Aero Sqn, USAS
F5946	— 148th Aero Sqn USAS
F5948	— 4 AFC Sqn; 148th Aero Sqn, USAS
F5950	— 46 Sqn & lost 1/10/18
F5951	— 17th Aero Sqn, USAS & lost 25/8/18
F5953	— 209 Sqn, Sep 1918
F5954	— 80 Sqn & crashed 2/10/18
F5958	— 3 Sqn RFC
F5959	— France
F5960	— France
F5966	— 213 Sqn
F5967	— 17th Aero Sqn, USAS
F5968	— 54 Sqn
F5969	— 17th Aero Sqn, USAS
F5972	— 201 Sqn
F5981	— France
F5983	— 148th Aero Sqn, USAS
F5985	— 17th Aero Sqn, USAS
F5990	— France
F5991	— 201 Sqn
F5993	— 17th Aero Sqn, USAS
F6022	— 'S' of 201 Sqn
F6024	— 17th Aero Sqn, USAS
F6026	— 80 Sqn & lost 1/20/18
F6027	— 203 Sqn
F6029	— 3 Sqn
F6030	— 209 Sqn

F6032	— 3 Sqn		F9632	— 43 TDS, Chattis Hill
F6033	— France		F9634	— 29 TDS, Beaulieu
F6034	— 'N' of 17th Aero Sqn, USAS		F9635	— CFS, Upavon
F6037	— 'FUMS UP' of 204 Sqn		F9637	— 42 Training Sqn
F6038	— 70 Sqn & crashed 2/10/18		F9657	— 209 Sqn
F6052	— 73 Sqn		F9695	— CFS, Upavon
F6053	— 73 Sqn			
F6058	— 148th Aero Sqn USAS		H6847	— France
F6063	— 73 Sqn		H6855	— 3 Sqn
F6064	— 54 Sqn		H6860	— France
F6084	— 151 Sqn; 152 Sqn;		H6997	— 209 Sqn
F6087	— 43 Sqn & lost 29/7/18		H7001	— 65 Sqn & lost 7/10/18
F6088	— 151 Sqn		H7003	— France
F6089	— 3 Sqn		H7007	— 65 Sqn (5-victories aircraft)
F6090	— 151 Sqn; 152 Sqn;		H7012	— France
F6102	— 151 Sqn; 152 Sqn;		H7089	— France
F6107	— 73 Sqn & lost 15/9/18		H7092	— France
F6109	— 73 Sqn		H7097	— Crashed 1 ARD 4/11/18
F6110	— 80 Sqn		H7098	— France
F6111	— 152 Sqn		H7107	— Crashed 1 ARD 30/10/18
F6117	— 3 Sqn		H7160	— France
F6122	— 152 Sqn		H7235	— 41st Aero Sqn, USAS
F6123	— 54 Sqn		H7238	— 4 AFC Sqn
F6132	— 54 Sqn		H7239	— France
F6135	— 148th Aero Sqn, USAS		H7262	— 54 Sqn
F6138	— 17th Aero Sqn, USAS		H7272	— 17th Aero Sqn, USAS
F6149	— 54 Sqn		H7278	— 209 & lost in air collision, 8/10/18
F6150	— 43 Sqn & lost 19/7/18		H7280	— 41st Aero Sqn, USAS
F6151	— 80 Sqn		H7281	— 17th Aero Sqn, USAS
F6152	— France		H7283	— 54 Sqn
F6153	— 65 Sqn		H7288	— 65 Sqn & lost 28/9/18
F6163	— 17th Aero Sqn, USAS		H7359	— 148th Aero Sqn, USAS
F6169	— 148th Aero Sqn, USAS		H8200	— 43 TDS, Chattis Hill
F6175	— 3 Sqn; 148th Aero Sqn, USAS		H8253	— 42 Training Sqn
F6176	— 148th Aero Sqn, USAS		H8258	— Built as 2-seater, 43 TDS, Chattis Hill
F6180	— 3 Sqn		H8259	— Built as 2-seater, 43 TDS, Chattis Hill
F6183	— France		H8260	— 43 TDS, Chattis Hill
F6185	— 148th Aero Sqn, USAS & lost 1/10/18		H8261	— 43 TDS, Chattis Hill
F6191	— France		H8262	— 43 TDS, Chattis Hill
F6192	— France		H8264	— CFS, Upavon
F6194	— 17th Aero Sqn, USAS		H8291	— CFS, Upavon
F6195	— 201 Sqn & lost 10/11/18		H8292	— CFS, Upavon
F6201	— 148th Aero Sqn, USAS			
F6210	— 46 Sqn; 17th Aero Sqn, USAS			
F6211	— 17th Aero Sqn, USAS			
F6221	— 201 Sqn		*KNOWN TWO-SEAT CONVERSIONS*	
F6223	— 'Y' of 201 Sqn			
F6240	— 'X' of B Flt, 201 Sqn		B2438	—
F6245	— France		B2504	—
F6249	— 17th Aero Sqn, USAS		B3801	— 110hp Le Rhone; first such conversion?
F6250	— 201 Sqn		B5575	— Shotwick, 1918
F6251	— 80 Sqn		B5713	— 204 TDS, Eastchurch
F6254	— 3 Sqn		B6218	—
F6257	— 210 Sqn		B6318	—
F6258	— 201 Sqn		B7219	—
F6259	— France		B7244	—
F6264	— France 201 Sqn		B7289	— Cranwell
F6271	— 3 Sqn		B7323	—
F6295	— France		B7371	—
F6303	— 3 Sqn		B7464	— Joyce Green
F9509	— 204 Sqn; 210 Sqn;		B7745	— Joyce Green
F9548	— 207 TDS, Chingford		B9140	—
F9579	— 204 TDS, Eastchurch		C19	—
F9623	— 6th Wing, Dover		C42	—
F9624	— 6th Wing, Dover		C57	— Eastbourne
F9628	— 3 TDS, Lopscombe Corner		E9968	— SEAFIS; rebuilt by 3 ARD
F9629	— 3 TDS, Lopscombe Corner		F1346	— France
F9630	— 3 TDS, Lopscombe Corner		F1946	— 5 AFC Training Sqn, Minchinhampton
F9631	— 43 TDS Chattis Hill		F4019	—
			H8258	— 43 TDS, Chattis Hill
			H8259	— 43 TDS, Chattis Hill

PRINCIPAL DIMENSIONS

	F.1 (130 hp Clerget)	2F.1 (130 hp Clerget)
Wing span (both planes	28 ft 0 in	26 ft 1 in
Chord (both planes	4 ft 6 in	4 ft 5 in
Chord of tailplane	3 ft 4½ in	3 ft 4½ in
Incidence (both planes)...	2-degrees	2-degrees
Gap at fuselage	5 ft 0 in	4 ft 11 in
Gap at outer struts	4 ft 2 in	4 ft 2 in
Gap at wingtips	4 ft 2 in	4 ft 2 in
Gap at wingtips	3 ft 10 in	3 ft 9 in
Dihedral, upper plane	Nil	Nil
Dihedral, lower plane	5-degrees	5½ degrees
Overall length **	18 ft 9 in	18 ft 9 in
Height	8 ft 6 in	8 ft 11½ in
Wheel track	4 ft 5¼ in	4 ft 5 in
Wheel diameter	2 ft 4 in	2 ft 4 in
Tailplane incidence (c/line)	1½-degrees	1½-degrees
Stagger at C/Section	1 ft 6 in	1 ft 5 in
Stagger at outer struts	1 ft 6 in	1 ft 5 in
Tail span	8 ft 2½ in	8 ft 2½ in
C/Section width	7 ft 3½ in	7 ft 3½ in
Airscrew diameter	8 ft 6 in	8 ft 5 in
Areas: Wing	231 sq ft	
Ailerons (each)	9 sq ft	
Tailpiece	14 sq ft	
Elevators	10½ sq ft	
Fin	3 sq ft	
Rudder	4.9 sq ft	

**F/n: Overall length varied slightly with engine installation:

150 hp BR1 & Monosoupape	18 ft 6 in
110 hp Le Rhone	18 ft 8 in
170 hp Le Rhone, 100 hp Mono, 150 hp Gnome.....	19 ft 0 in

Fuel/Oil Tankage:	Main (pressure) fuel tank	30 galls
	Gravity fuel	7 galls
	Oil	6½ galls

COSTS

Sopwith F.1

Airframe, less engine, instruments & guns	£874.10. 0d
130 hp Clerget engine	£907.10. 0d
110 hp Le Rhone engine	£771.10. 0d
100 hp Gnome Monosoupape engine	£696. 0. 0d
150 hp BR1 engine	£643.10. 0d

Sopwith 2F.1

Airframe, less engine, instruments & guns	£825. 0. 0d

WEIGHT & PERFORMANCES

	F.1/1	F.1/3	F.1/3	F.1/3	B2312
	130 Clerget	130 Clerget	140 Clerget	110 Le Rhone	130 Clerget
Max speeds (mph):					
At 6,500 ft	-	-	-	-	108
At 10,000 ft	112.5	113	-	108.5	104.5
At 15,000 ft	106	106.5	113.5	103	97.5
Climb to (mins/secs):					
6,500 ft	6.00	6.00	5.00	5.15	6.40
10,000 ft	10.35	10.35	8.30	9.00	11.45
15,000 ft	21.5	20.40	15.45	17.20	23.15
Service ceiling (ft):	19,000	19,000	24,000	21,000	18,500
Endurance (hrs):	2¾	2½	-	2¾	-
Weights (lb):					
Empty	950	929	-	889	962
Military load	100	101	101	101	101
Crew	180	180	180	180	180
Fuel/Oil	252	243	-	238	239
Fully loaded	1,482	1,453	1,452	1,408	1,422

B3829	B3835	B3811	F6394	N518	2-Seat	F1336	F1515	B3862
110 Le Rhone	150 BR1	100 Mono	170 Le Rhone	150 BR1	110 Le Rhone	150 Mono	150 Gnome	130 Clerget
-	-	-	-	116.5	-	-	-	107
-	121	110.5	113	111	103	117.5	-	102.5
111.5	114.5	102.5	108.5	103	-	107	-	93
5.10	4.35	6.50	5.30	5.30	10.35	-	6.42	-
9.10	8.20	11.50	9.35	9.50	18.55	10.15	11.24	16.40
16.50	15.55	23.15	17.30	20	41.30	19.40	18.45	33.25
24,000	22.000	18,500	21,500	18,000	-	21.450	23,000	20,500
-	2½	2¾	-	2½	-	-	-	-
-	-	882	1,048	977	889	1,062	987	-
101	101	101	101	101	Nil	101	70	101
180	180	180	180	180	360	180	165	180
-	-	224	238	250	159	180	237	-
1,422	1,470	1,387	1,567	1,508	1,408	1,523	1,459	1,524

SOPWITH BIPLANE F. 1.
(130 H.P. CLERGET.)

TRUING UP FUSELAGE (see Fig. 1).

The Side Struts are numbered from front to rear of Machine. Support the Fuselage on two trestles one placed under the first bay and the other under the last bay.

Starting at No. 1 vertical Side Strut mark points on consecutive Vertical Side Struts $15\frac{1}{4}''$, $15\frac{1}{4}''$, $15\frac{1}{4}''$, $15\frac{1}{4}''$, $15\frac{1}{16}''$, $13\frac{17}{32}''$, $11\frac{5}{16}''$, $9\frac{1}{2}''$, $7\frac{5}{32}''$, respectively below the *upper surface* of the Top Longerons. These marked points must be along the Thrust Line in Side elevation when Fuselage is trued up.

Lightly clamp a straightedge tranversely across No. 3 Side Struts, the marked points to be on the *upper edge*.

Lightly clamp small blocks of wood at all other marked points, the marks to be on the *upper edge* of the blocks.

Proceed to true up as follows :

Tension Internal Cross Bracing Wires until diagonals are equal in each section. Check by trammel.

Make Top Cross Bracing Wires equal in each bay and similarly make Bottom Cross Bracing Wires equal in each bay. Check by trammel.

Level the transverse straightedge by suitably packing up the front support.

Adjust the Side Bracing Wires on one side until any two consecutive marked points on Vertical Side Struts are in a horizontal line and all Struts are vertical.

Check the former by placing a straightedge across consecutive blocks and adjust until the straightedge is level and check the latter by plumbing each Strut.

Proceed similarly on the other side.

The Sternpost should be vertical viewed from any direction when the Fuselage is trued up.

TRUING UP UNDERCARRIAGE (see Fig. 2).

The Undercarriage is trued up by making Diagonal Bracing Wires equal in length. Check by trammel.

PLACING MACHINE IN FLYING POSITION.

Before truing up the Centre Section and fitting the Main Planes it is necessary to get the Machine in Flying Position.

To do this support the Machine by blocks placed under the Undercarriage Struts and on a trestle placed under the Tail. The Machine is in Flying Position when the Front Spar at the Bottom of the Fuselage to which the Front Spars of the Lower Main Planes are attached, is level transversely and when the Top Longerons in the Pilot's Cockpit are level longitudinally. Level longitudinally by raising or lowering Tail and transversely by packing blocks under the Undercarriage Struts.

TRUING UP THE CENTRE SECTION (See Figs. 2 and 3).

The Centre Section is symmetrical about the vertical centre line of Machine. True up by Centre Section Cross Bracing Wires and ensure that both Upper Wires are equal in length and also that both Lower Wires are equal in length.

The *Stagger* of the Centre Section is $18''$. This can be adjusted by the Stagger Wires *after* the Lower Main Planes have been fitted.

Check by dropping plumb lines from the Leading Edges of the Centre Section ; the *fore* and *aft* horizontal distance of the Leading Edge of the Lower Main Planes should be $18''$ from the plumb lines.

ATTACHING THE MAIN PLANES.

Place the Lower Main Planes in position and insert the Securing Rod on each side from the *rear*.

Push the latter Rod well in and secure it to the *Ribs* at the Roots of the Main Planes by nuts and bolts, not forgetting to insert the *Split Pins*.

Loosely connect the Landing Wires.

Lift the Upper Main Planes in position, insert the Securing Rods from the *front* and after pushing the Rods well in, secure the front of the Rods to the Leading Edges of the Main Planes.

Loosely connect Flying and Incidence Wires.

TRUING UP MAIN PLANES.

Drop plumb lines from four points, two each side, on the Leading Edge of the Upper Main Planes. True up until—

(a) The plumb lines are in line viewed from the side.

(b) The Leading Edge of the Upper Main Planes is straight viewed from the front and in plan view, there being no *Dihedral* on the Upper Main Planes.

(c) The Leading Edge of the Lower Main Planes is symmetrical about centre line of Machine.
Check by taking measurements from Bottom Sockets of Front Outer Struts to Rudderpost and Propeller Boss. Corresponding measurements should be the same on both sides.

(a) The *Dihedral* of the Lower Main Planes is $5°$. Check by Abney level and straightedge along the Front and Rear Spars.

(e) The *Incidence* is 2° throughout. Check by Abney level and straightedge, taking care to place the latter from Leading Edge to Trailing Edge at *Ribs*.

(f) The *Stagger* is 18″ at *Centre Section* and 18$\frac{5}{16}$″ at *Outer Struts*. Check by measuring the *fore* and *aft* horizontal distance from the Leading Edge of the Lower Main Planes to the plumb lines dropped from the Leading Edge of the Upper Main Planes.

(g) There is no "*Wash In*" or "*Wash Out*."

FIXING THE EMPENNAGE. (See Figs. 3 and 4).

Bolt the Tail Plane in position and connect the Tail Plane Bracing Wires

True up the Tail Plane to be level transverely.

Check by spirit level along the Front Spar and along the Hinged Tube.

Check for Tail Plane being square with Machine by taking measurements from Bottom Sockets of Rear Outer Struts to lateral extremities of Rear Spar of Tail Plane.

These measurements should be the same on both sides.

The *Incidence* of the Tail Plane is 1½°. Check by using a straightedge with two small blocks attached. These blocks should be of such dimensions that when one is on the Front Spar and the other on the Hinged Tube of the Tail Plane, the *upper edge* of the straightedge is parallel to the *fore* and *aft* centre line of the Tail Plane.

The *Incidence* can be measured by an Abney level over the straightedge with Machine in flying Position.

Bolt the Fin in Position

Hinge the Rudder to the Sternpost and Fin, not forgetting to insert the Split Pins, similarly hinge the Elevators to the Rear Spar of Tail Plane.

NOTE.—The two Elevators should be rigidly connected, so that if the Elevator Control is damaged on one side the Elevators can be operated from the other side.

CONTROLS.

Connect up the Controls and adjust them so that

(a) With the Pilot's Control Stick central there is no *Droop* on the Ailerons.

(b) When the upper *front edge* of the tubular reinforcement on the Pilots Control Stick just beneath the handle is 9$\frac{3}{4}$″ *horizontally in rear* of the Dashboard, the Elevators are in continuation of the Tail Plane.

(c) The Rudder and Tail Skid point directly *fore* and *aft* and are square with Machine when the Rudder Bar is square in Fuselage.

POINTS TO OBSERVE WHEN OVERHAULING MACHINE.

See that the Leading Edges of the Main Planes are symmetrical, about centre line of Machine.

Check the Stagger.

Examine the Bracing Wires for length and tautness in the Centre Section, and see that the Split Pins are in position, and that all Lock Nuts are tight.

Check the Dihedral of Lower Main Planes.

Check the Incidence.

See that the Interplane Struts are straight.

Examine all Main Plane Bracing Wires for length and tautness, and see that all Split Pins are in position.

Examine all Controls, Control Pulleys and Cables, see that they work freely and that Turnbuckles on Cables are locked.

Examine Tail Plane and see that it is set correctly and is square with Machine, and that all Tail Plane Bracing Wires are correct both as to tautness and length, and that all Split Pins are in position, and that all Lock Nuts are tight.

Examine Rudder and Fin and see that they are set straight and square with Machine.

Measure the Droop of the Ailerons and Elevators.

Examine Undercarriage and Skid.

Examine Tank Mountings and Connections.

Examine Engine Mounting, Engine Controls, and Engine Accessories.

Examine Cartridge Drums and see that they are secure and do not foul the Carburetter.

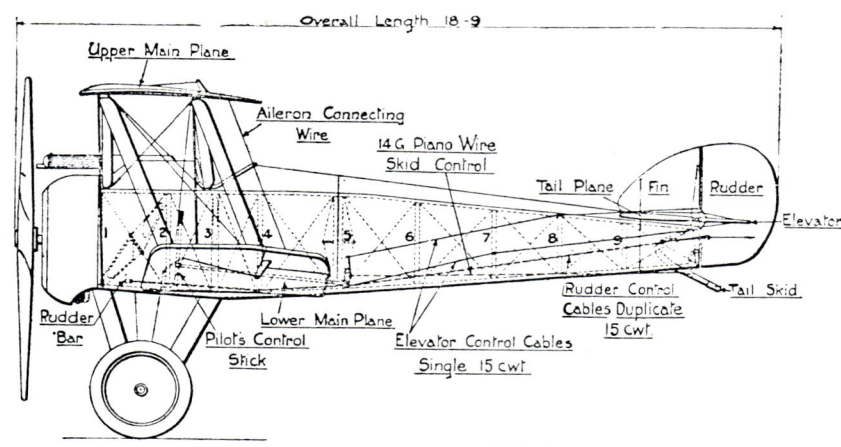

Overall Length 18·9

Upper Main Plane
Aileron Connecting Wire
14 G Piano Wire Skid Control
Tail Plane | Fin | Rudder
Elevator
Rudder Bar
Pilot's Control Stick
Lower Main Plane
Elevator Control Cables Single 15 cwt
Rudder Control Cables Duplicate 15 cwt
Tail Skid

FIG 1.
SIDE ELEVATION.

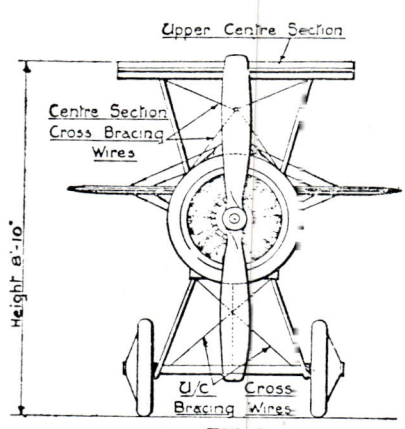

Upper Centre Section
Centre Section Cross Bracing Wires
Height 8'·10'
U/c Cross Bracing Wires

FIG 2
FRONT ELEVATION
(LESS MAIN PLANES)

Flying Position.

The Machine is in Flying Position when the Front Spar at the Bottom of the Fuselage is level transversely and when the Top Longerons in the Pilot's Cockpit are level longitudinally.

Truing up Fuselage.

Starting at Nº 1 vertical Side Strut mark points on consecutive vertical Side Struts 15½, 15¼, 15¼, 15¼, 15⅛, 13³²/₃₂, 11⅛, 9⅜ 7⁵³/₃₂ respectively below the upper surface of the Top Longerons also mark a point on the Sternpost 6' below the upper surface of the ends of the Top Longerons. These marked points should be along the Thrust line in Side Elevation when Fuselage is trued up. ·Lightly clamp a straightedge transversely across Nº 3 Side Struts the marked points to be on the upper edge. Lightly clamp small blocks of wood at all other marked points, the marks to be on the upper edge of the blocks.

Proceed to true up as follows. Tension Internal Cross Bracing Wires until diagonals are equal in each section Check by trammel. Make Top Cross Bracing Wires equal in each bay and similarly make Bottom Cross Bracing Wires equal in bay. Check by trammel. Level the transverse straightedge by suitably packing up the front support. Adjust the Side Bracing Wires on one side until any two consecutive marked points on vertical Side Struts are in a horizontal line and all Struts are vertical. Check the former by placing a straightedge across consecutive blocks and adjust until the straightedge is level and check the latter by plumbing each Strut Proceed similarly on the other side. The Sternpost should be vertical viewed from any direction when the Fuselage is trued up.

Truing up Undercarriage

The Undercarriage is trued up by making Cross Bracing Wires equal in length. Check by trammel.

Truing up Centre Section

The Centre Section is symmetrical about the vertical centre line of Machine True up by Centre Section Cross Bracing Wires and ensure that both Upper Wires are equal in length and also- that both Lower Wires are equal in length. The Stagger of the Centre Section is 18' This can be adjusted by the Centre Section Side Bracing Wires after the Lower Main Planes have been fitted. Check by dropping plumb lines from the Leading Edge of the Upper Centre Section Plane. The fore and aft horizontal distance of the Leading Edge of the Lower Main Planes should be 18' from the plumb lines.

FRONT ELEVATION

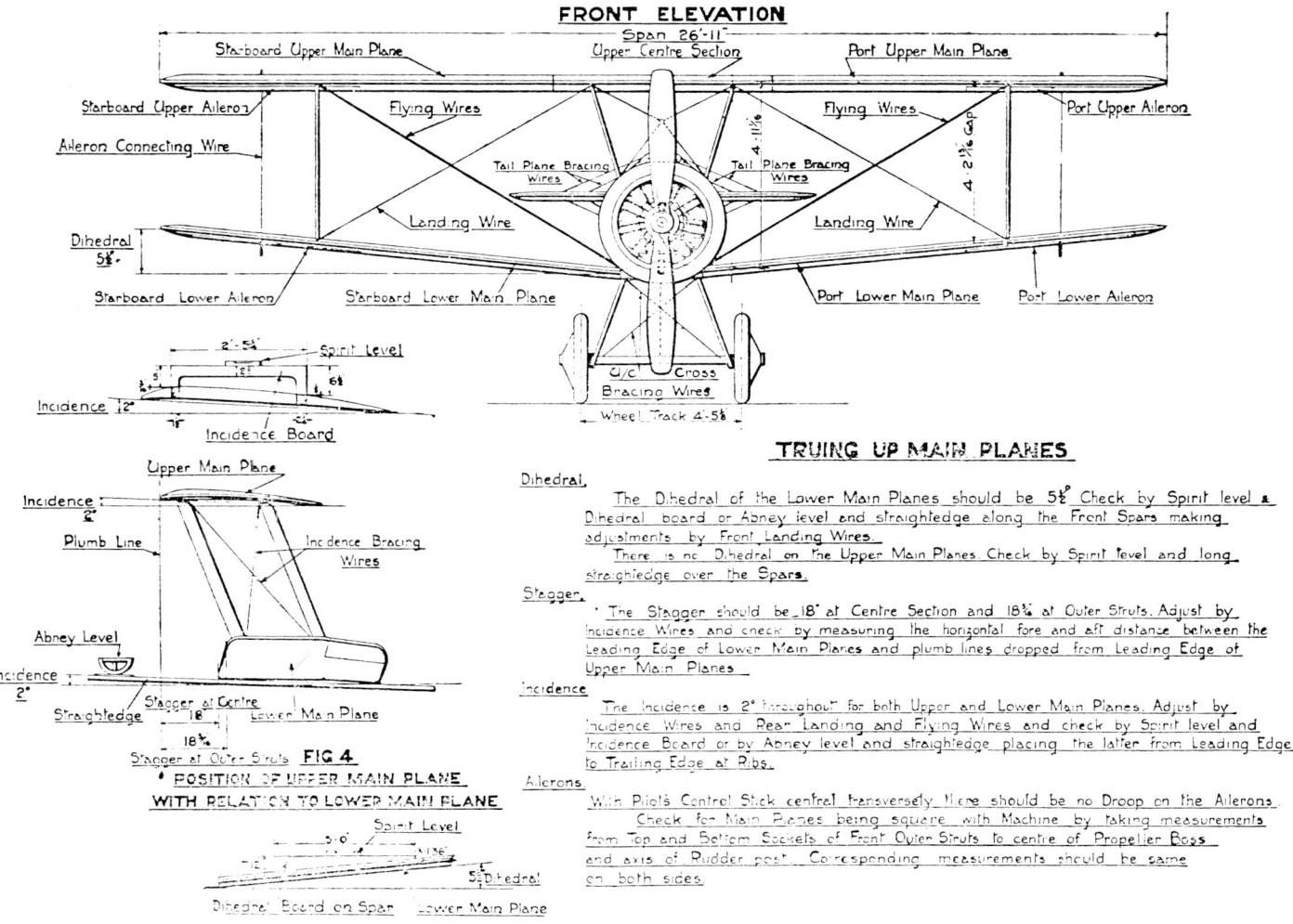

Span 26'-11"

Starboard Upper Main Plane · Upper Centre Section · Port Upper Main Plane

Starboard Upper Aileron — Flying Wires — Flying Wires — Port Upper Aileron

Aileron Connecting Wire

Tail Plane Bracing Wires · Tail Plane Bracing Wires

Landing Wire · Landing Wire

Dihedral 5½°

Starboard Lower Aileron · Starboard Lower Main Plane · Port Lower Main Plane · Port Lower Aileron

A/C Cross Bracing Wires

Wheel Track 4'-5½"

Spirit Level · Incidence 2° · Incidence Board

Upper Main Plane

Incidence 2° · Plumb Line · Incidence Bracing Wires

Abney Level

Incidence 2° · Straightedge · Stagger at Centre 18" · Lower Main Plane

18¼"

Stagger at Outer Struts **FIG 4**

POSITION OF UPPER MAIN PLANE WITH RELATION TO LOWER MAIN PLANE

Spirit Level

5½° Dihedral

Dihedral Board on Spar · Lower Main Plane

TRUING UP MAIN PLANES

Dihedral.

    The Dihedral of the Lower Main Planes should be 5½° Check by Spirit level & Dihedral board or Abney level and straightedge along the Front Spars making adjustments by Front Landing Wires.

    There is no Dihedral on the Upper Main Planes. Check by Spirit level and long straightedge over the Spars.

Stagger.

    The Stagger should be 18" at Centre Section and 18¼" at Outer Struts. Adjust by Incidence Wires and check by measuring the horizontal fore and aft distance between the Leading Edge of Lower Main Planes and plumb lines dropped from Leading Edge of Upper Main Planes.

Incidence.

    The Incidence is 2° throughout for both Upper and Lower Main Planes. Adjust by Incidence Wires and Rear Landing and Flying Wires and check by Spirit level and Incidence Board or by Abney level and straightedge placing the latter from Leading Edge to Trailing Edge at Ribs.

Ailerons.

    With Pilot's Control Stick central transversely there should be no Droop on the Ailerons.

    Check for Main Planes being square with Machine by taking measurements from Top and Bottom Sockets of Front Outer Struts to centre of Propeller Boss and axis of Rudder post. Corresponding measurements should be same on both sides.

GENERAL PLAN

EMPENNAGE

Tail Plane

The centre line of Tail Plane should first be set at an Incidence of 1½°. In this position the distance between top of Top Longerons and the undersurface of Rear Spar Tube should be 1⅝". Adjustments by means of Nut & Screw at Rear Spar Tube can be made after trials.

The Tail Plane should be level transversely and square with Machine. Check by taking measurements from tops of Side Struts No 7 to lateral extremities of Rear Spar of Tail Plane. Corresponding measurements should be the same on both sides (i.e. X - X')

EMPENNAGE (cont)

Elevators

With top of Pilots Control Stick 10½"(±½) horizontally in rear of Dashboard the Elevators should be in direct continuation of Tail Plane.

Fin

This should point directly fore and aft and be square with Machine.

Rudder & Tail Skid.

With Rudder Bar square in Fuselage the Rudder & Tail Skid should point directly fore and aft and be square with Machine

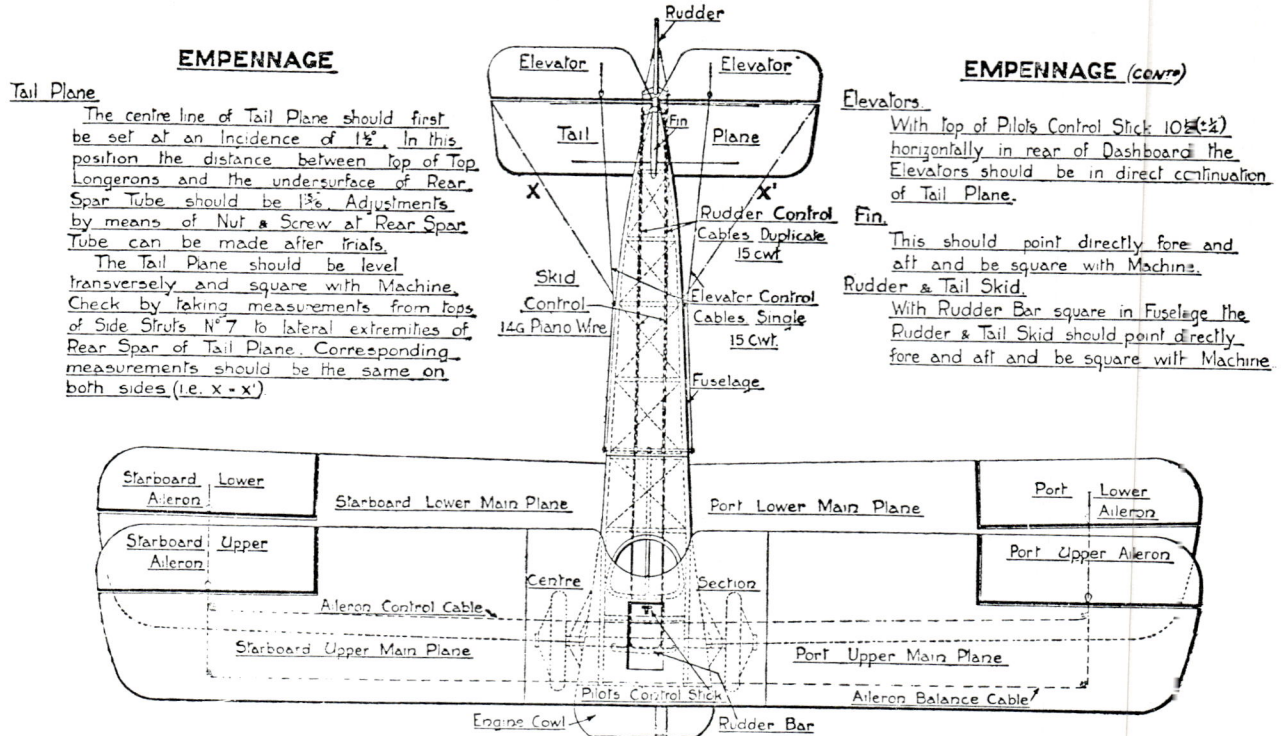

RAF — WIRE LENGTHS

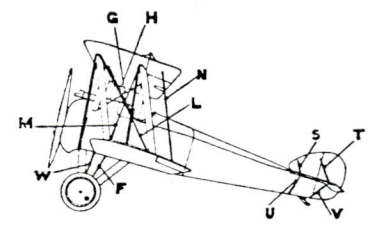

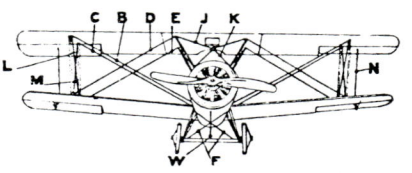

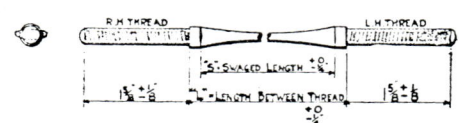

Description	N°Off	Index	L	S	Size	Remarks
Fuselage Tie (Front)	2	A	1'- 6"	1 - 5⅛	¼ BSF	
Front Flying Wires	4	B	9 - 0¼	8 - 11⅝	"	
Rear Flying Wires	4	C	9 - 0⅝	9 - 0¼	"	
Front Landing Wire	2	D	7'- 9¾	7'- 9⅜	"	
Rear Landing Wire	2	E	"	"	"	
Undercarriage Cross Bracing Wire	2	F	3'- 4½	3'- 4⅛	"	
Centre Section Side Bracing (Short)	2	G	2'- 10	2'- 9½	"	
Centre Section Side Bracing (Long)	2	H	3'- 2⅞	3'- 2⅝	2 BA	
Front Centre Section Cross Bracing (Top)	2	J	1'- 7⅝	1'- 7½	¼ BSF	Use AGS Forkends
Front Centre Section " (Bottom)	2	K	1'- 6⅜	1'- 5⅞	"	" " " "
Incidence Wire (Long)	2	L	5'- 1	5-0½	2BA	
Incidence Wire (Short)	2	M	3'- 9¾	3-8⅞	"	
Aileron Connecting Wire	2	N	3'- 11⅜	3'- 11	"	
Engine Bracing (Top)	2	O	" - 10⅞	" - 10⅜	"	
Engine Bracing (Bottom)	2	P	9⅝	8¾	"	
Main Drag Wire	2	Q	2'- 9	2- 8⅜	"	Internal Wing Bracing
Second Drag Wire	2	R	2'- 11"	2'- 10⅜	"	" " "
Tail Plane Bracing Wire (Top Front)	2	S	1'- 10⅜	1'- 10	"	
Tail Plane Bracing Wire (Top Rear)	2	T	2'- 8½	2'- 8⅜	"	
Tail Plane Bracing Wire (Bottom Front)	2	U	1'- 9½	1'- 9⅜	"	
Tail Plane Bracing Wire (Bottom Rear)	2	V	2'- 8⅝	2'- 8	"	
Undercarriage Centre Wire	1	W	3'- 1¼	3- 0⅝	¼ BSF	
Fuselage Tie (Rear)	1	X	5⅝		2BA	Round

HEIGHTS OF TOP LONGERONS
ABOVE THRUST LINE
MEASURED TO UPPER SURFACE

Vertical Side Strut are numbered from Front to Rear of Machine

Vertical Side Struts Number	Height of Top of Longerons above Thrust Line
1	15½
2	15¼
3	15¼
4	15¼
5	15⅛
6	13¹³⁄₃₂
7	11¹⁵⁄₁₆
8	9½
9	7⁷⁄₃₂
Sternpost	6

154.

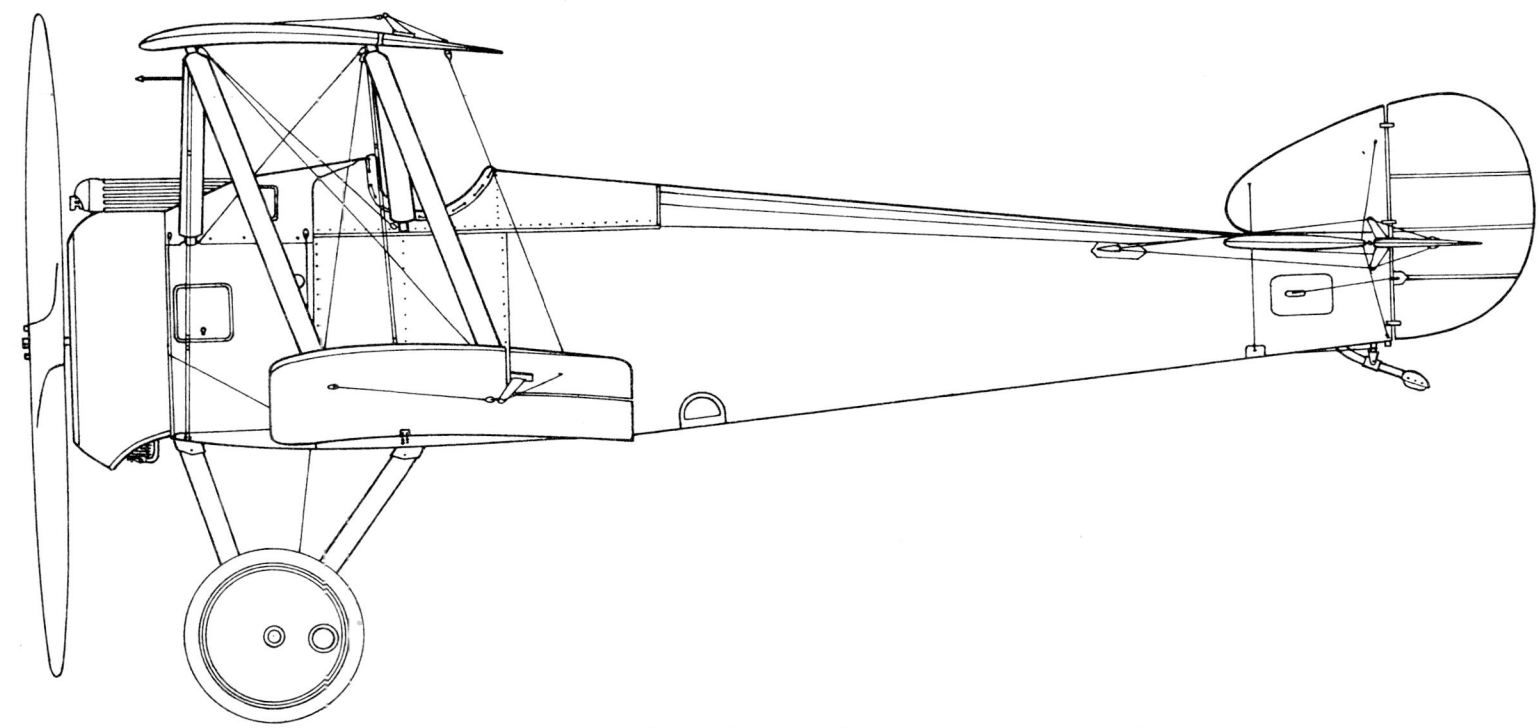

Original Sopwith F.1 Prototype (110hp Clerget 9z).

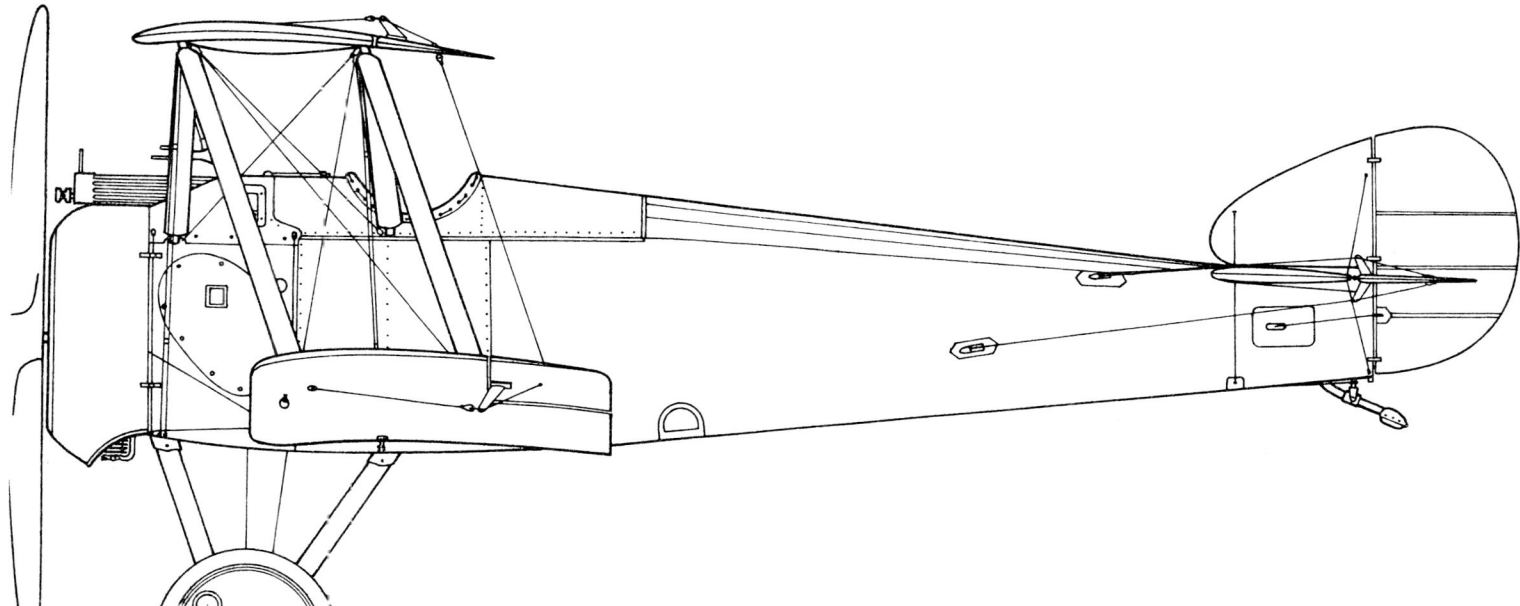

Production F.1 Camel

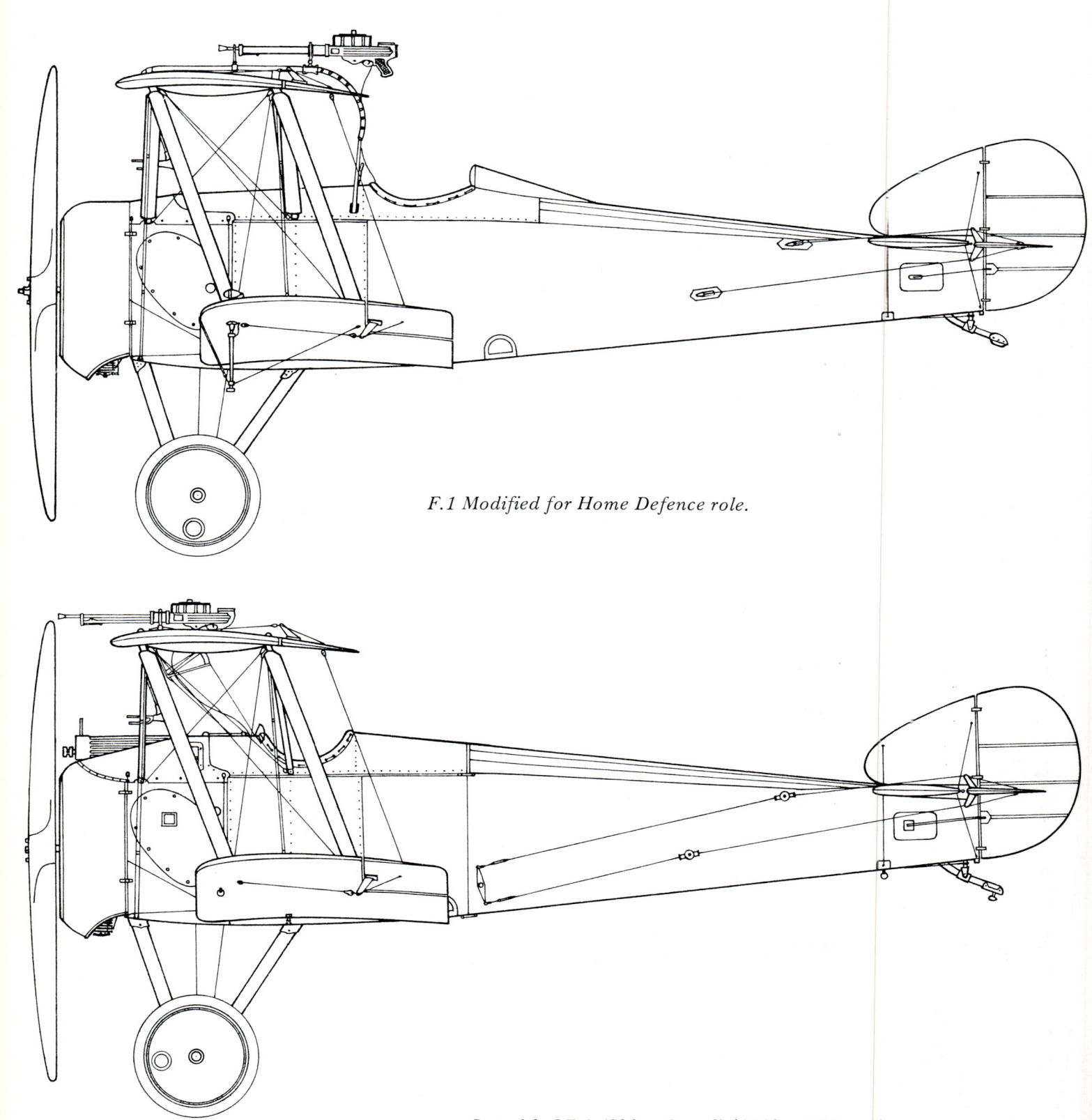

F.1 Modified for Home Defence role.

Sopwith 2F.1 'Ships Camel' (150hp BR1 engine ; one Vickers/one Lewis mg.

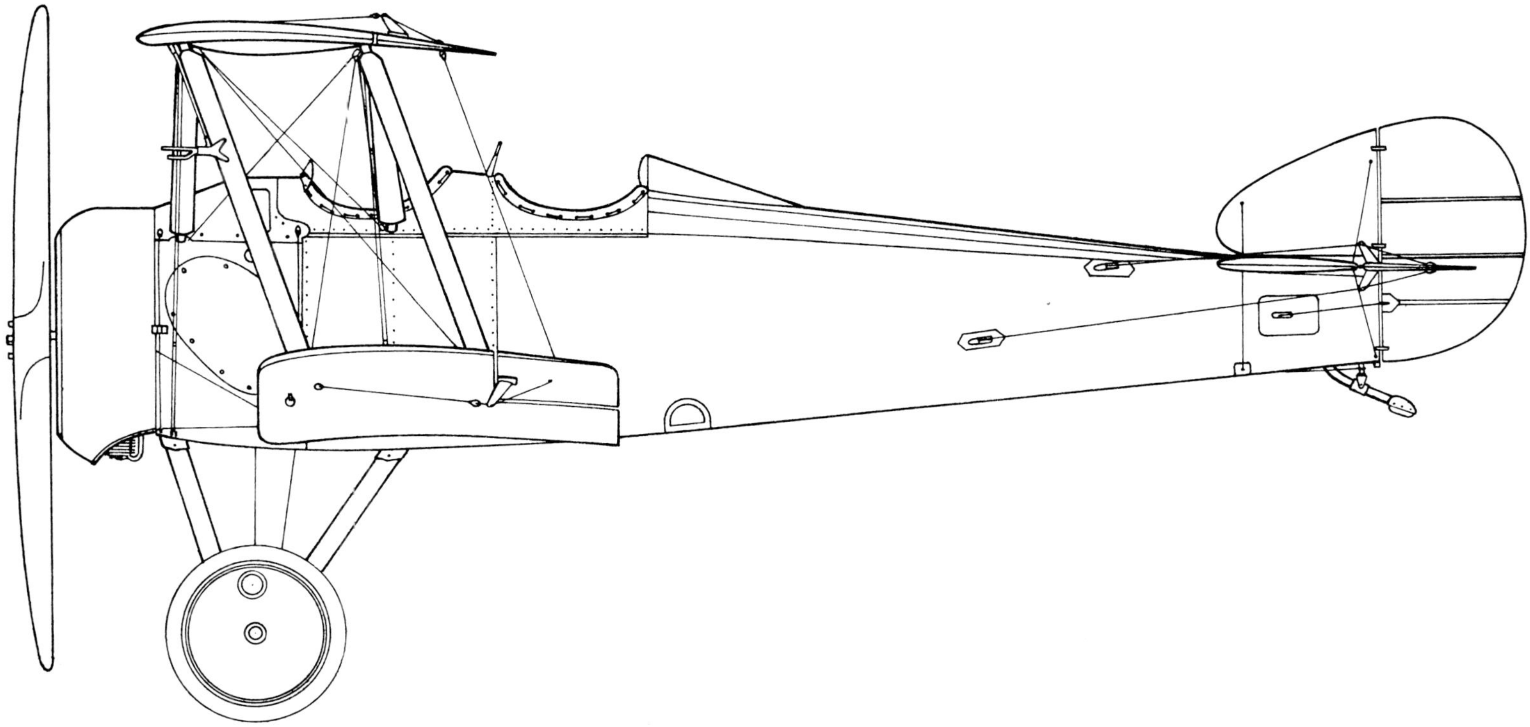

Sopwith F.1 Camel—converted to two-seat trainer (130hp Clerget 9b engine)

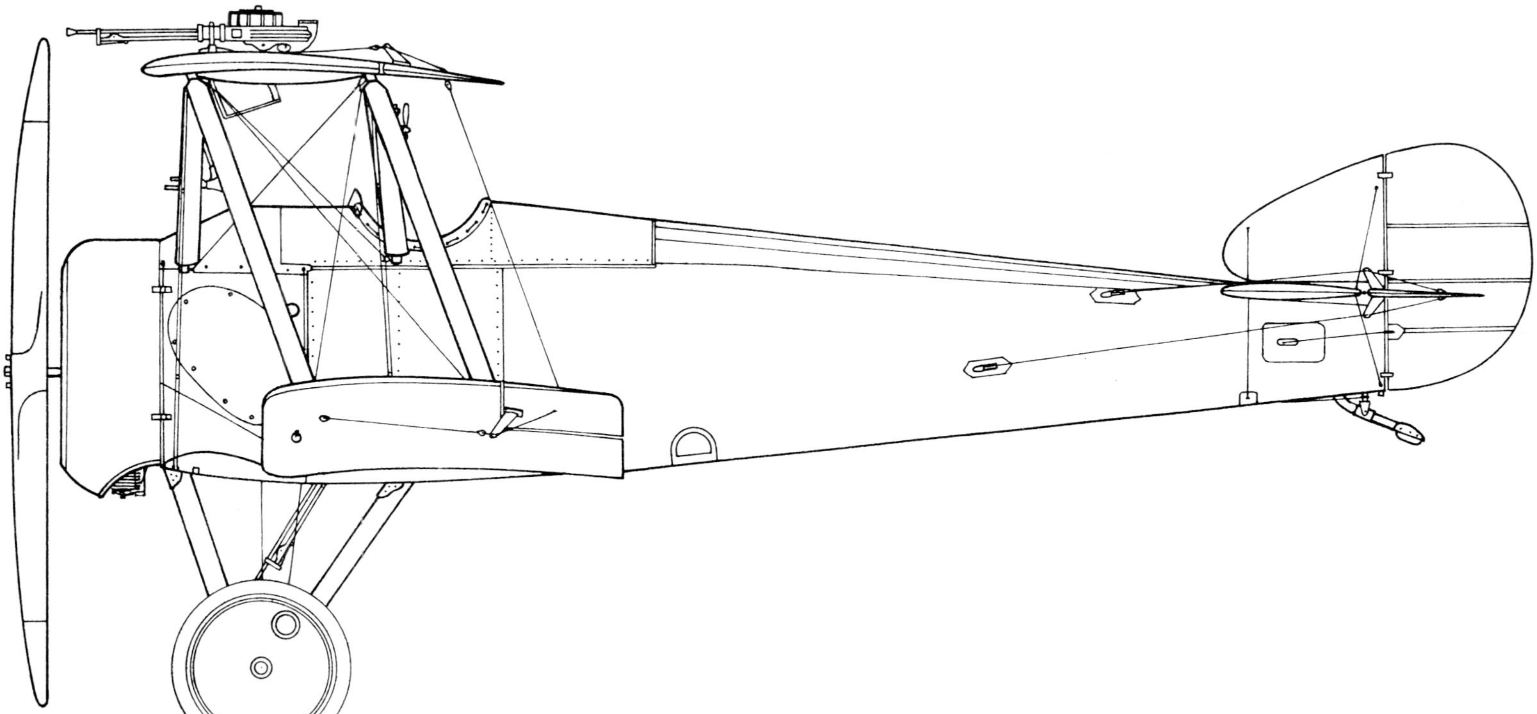

Sopwith TF.1 Camel ('Trench Fighter')—110hp Le Rhone 9 Twin Lewis mgs firing through under-fuselage, plus one Lewis above upper wing c/section.

SERVICE USE, 1916—18

Western Front:

RFC Squadrons: 3, 28, 43, 45, 46, 54, 65, 70, 73, 80, 151, 152.

RNAS Squadrons: 1, 3, 4, 6, 8, 9, 10, 13.

RAF Squadrons: 3, 43, 45, 46, 54, 65, 70, 73, 80, 151, 152, 201, 203, 204, 208, 209, 210, 213.

Australian FC: (Formerly 71 Sqn RFC)

USAS Squadrons: 17th, 41st, 148th, 185th.

Belgian AF: 1st, 4th, 6th, 11th Squadrons

Italian Front

RFC/RAF Squadrons: 28, 45, 66.

Mediterranean

Adriatic Group: Squadrons 224; 225 (482 Flt), Otranto; 226 Taranto; 227

Aegean Groups: Squadrons 220 (475, 476, 477 Flts); 222 (478, 479, 480 Flts); 223 C Squadron RNAS, Gliki; D Squadron RNAS Stavros; F Squadron, Thermi/Mudros; Royal Hellenic Air Service.

Macedonia

RFC/RAF Squadrons: 17, 47, 150 (C Flt only), 221

Mesopotamia

RFC/RAF Squadrons: 47 (B Flt only), 221, RAF Contingent, Archangel

UK HOME DEFENCE

RFC/RAF Squadrons: 37, 44, 50, 51, 61, 78, 112, 143, 212, 219 (470 Flt), 230 (487 Flt), 233 (471 Flt), 273 (485 and 486 Flts), plus various RNAS stations.

UK TRAINING

Units/Stations: 5 (AFC) TS, Minchinhampton; 6 (AFC) TS; 10 TS, Gosport; 31 TS, Wyton; 42 TS, Wye; 63 TS, Joyce Green; 94 (R) Sqn (Canadian); 188 NFTS; 189 NFTS; 6th Wing, Dover; 23rd Trng Wing, South Carlton (inc Scampton); 3 TDS, Lopscombe Corner; 29 TDS. Beaulieu 43 TDS, Chattis Hill; 204 TDS. Eastchurch; 207 TDS, Chingford; RNAS War School, Manston; Gosport School of Special Flying; AAFS, Lympne; Schools of Aerial Fighting at Ayr, Frieston, Marske, Sedgeford, Turnberry; Flying instructors' schools at Curragh, Lilbourne, Redcar, Shoreham; CFS, Upavon; Biggin Hill, Cranwell; Eastbourne; Harling Road; Leighterton (AFC); Tern Hill; Weston-on-Green.

CAMEL DISTRIBUTION, OCTOBER 31st, 1918

	150 BR1	Clerget	Le Rhone/Mono
United Kingdom			
In transit to/at ARD's	1	72	14
In store	84	160	127
At AAP's/Contractors	-	25	119
Areas	28	329	29
Schools	1	142	3
6th Brigade	-	-	181
Sundry Units	1	13	-
Central Transit Depot	5	13	10
Grand Fleet	26	4	10
Expeditionary Forces			
BEF, France	186	344	272
Independent Force, France	-	27	-
14th Wing, Italy	-	75	-
5th Group	24	12	-
Eastern Stations			
A/w shipment/assembly/in transit	-	26	25
Egypt/Palestine	-	-	9
Salonika	-	-	11
Mesopotamia	-	-	11
Mediterranean, various	-	100	-
TOTALS	356	1,342	821
Written-off charge, October	64	119	75

B9268, an F.1 which served with the 17th Aero Squadron, USAS, before being returned to the UK as a training machine. Here the twin Vickers guns have been replaced by a Hythe Camera Gun.

CAMEL SQUADRONS , NOVEMBER 11, 1918

No.	Location	Commanding Officer	Remarks
3	Inchy	Maj R St Clair McClintock	
4 AFC	Ennetieres	Maj W A McClaughry, MC, DFC	
28	Treviso	Maj W J Guilfoyle	
37	Stow Maries	Maj F W Honnett	7 Camels/6 SE5a
43	Bouvincourt	Maj C C Miles, MC	
44	Hainault Farm	Maj A T Harris	HD: 19 Camels
45	Bettoncourt	Maj A M Miller, DSO	Attached I.F.
46	Busigny	Maj G Allen	
50	Bekesbourne	Maj W Sowrey	HD
54	Merchin	Maj R S Maxwell, MC	
61	Rochford	Maj E B Mason	HD
65	Bisseghem	Maj H V C de Crespigny, MC, DFC	
66	San Pietro-in-Gu	Maj I T Whittaker, MC	
70	West Halluih	Maj G W Murlis-Green, DSO, MC	
73	Hervilly	Maj M le Blanc-Smith, DFC	
78	Suttons Farm	Maj C J Truran	HD: 20 Camels
80	Bertry West	Maj D V Bell	
112	Throwley	Maj C O Usborne	HD: 20 Camels
143	Detling	Maj F Sowrey, DSO, MC	HD
150	Kirec	Maj W R B McBain, MC	Flt at Marian
151	Bancourt	Maj C J Q Brand, DSO, MC, DFC	Nightfighters
152	Carvin	Maj E Henty	Nightfighters
188	Throwley	Maj C B Cooke	HD training
189	Suttons Farm	Maj H S Powell, MC	HD training
198	Rochford	Capt L F Beyman	HD training
201	La Targette	Maj C M Leman	
203	Bruille	Maj T F Hazell, DSO, MC, DFC	
204	Courtrai	Maj E W Norton, DSC	
208	Maretz	Maj C Draper, DSC	
209	Bruille	Maj T F N Gerrard, DSC	
210	Boussieres	Maj B C Bell, DSO, DSC	
213	Berques	Maj R Graham, DSC	
185th Aero, USAS	Rembercourt	Capt J C Vasconcelles	Nightfighters

NB: This list does not include the many units having a few Camels on strength for 'internal' escort role — particularly ex-RNAS units in Middle East zones.

VICTORY CLAIMS

To dogmatize about specific figures relating to fighter pilots' 'scores' is both unwise and — to many historians — pointless. Nevertheless, it is logical to a certain extent to measure such pilots' prowess by comparison of claimed victories. All totals listed below are those positively claimed and confirmed under the contemporary rulings for 'victories'. Each is supported by an official combat report. Each total is a minimum; all doubtful claims have been omitted, and only officially sponsored claims are included. It should be emphasised that a 'victory' did not necessarily equate with an enemy aircraft destroyed; the bulk of confirmed 'victories' during 1914-18, for all nations, came into the category 'Out of Control'; whereby an enemy machine was seen to go down, apparently completely defeated, but whose ultimate fate was not witnessed. Many individual claims have been omitted for lack of corroborative evidence and/or documentation; while other isolated victories, though confirmed as such, are not included here e.g the Zeppelin L.53 destroyed by S D Culley, and a Gotha destroyed by an RNAS Camel pilot from RNAS Westgate. These 'one-off' claims are quoted appropriately within the main narrative of this book. Exhaustive comparisons of victory claims by pilots of other types of single-seat fighting aircraft, of all nations, during the 1914-18 aerial conflict, show unequivocally the Sopwith Camel's premier claim as the war's most destructive fighter plane.

CAMEL UNIT CLAIMS

Squadron	Destroyed	KB's	Captured	Out of Control	Totals
3	34	6	2	43	85
28	108	13	-	20	141
43	78	9	1	50	138
44	1	-	-	-	1
45	143	-	1	72	216
46	73	7	-	72	152
54	52	2	1	17	72
65	95	1	1	85	182
66	132	18	-	17	167
70	128	5	1	98	232
73	83	-	-	38	121
80	25	2	-	15	42
112	1	-	-	-	1
151	20	-	-	1	21
150	7	-	-	7	14
1 (N)/201	75	8	-	85	168
3 (N)/203	70+	1	-	52	123+
4 (N)/204	70	3	-	102	175
6 (N)	6	-	-	6	12
8 (N)/208	53	3	-	109	165
9 (N)/209	58	-	2	34	94
10 (N)/210	86	6	-	59	151
13 (N)/213	61	3	-	30	94
17th Aero USAS	30	3	-	21	54 -
148th Aero USAS	34	?	-	?	65
4 AFC	120	30	1	53	204
TOTALS	1,543	120	10	1,086	2,790

'ACE CAMELS'

Particular aircraft were seldom allocated to individual pilots — Major W G Barker's B6313 being an outstanding exception — due to the varying circumstances of maintenance, attrition and availability. Nevertheless, a number of prominent Camel pilots did fly specific machines for several weeks, even months, of operations, and accumulated reasonably high victory scores in certain Camels. The following table, though by no means claimed to be comprehensive, lists 67 Camels in which it is positively known that five or more victories were claimed by their pilots. The final column indicates the overall score achieved by each particular Camel; and, where known, the pilot responsible is named. Figures in brackets following a pilot's name indicate that pilot's specific 'share' of the aircraft total score.

B6313	Maj W G Barker	28, 66, 139 Sqns	41+	C8240	Lt H C Daniels	43 Sqn	6
D3417	Maj R Collishaw	203 Sqn	17+	C8270	Capt J Trollope	43 Sqn	6
D6402	Capt H W Woollett	43 Sqn	17+	D1817	Lt T Williams (5)	65 Sqn	6
B7220	Capt A T Whealey (12)	203 Sqn	14	D1864	Capt C F King	43 Sqn	6
D6418	Capt D R McLaren	46 Sqn	14	D3332	Various	210 Sqn	6
D1961	Capt E J K McCloughry	4 AFC Sqn	13	D3374	Lt W B Craig	204 Sqn	6
B7475	Capt F G Quigley	70 Sqn	12	D6603	Capt D R McLaren	46 Sqn	6
C8278	Capt J Gilmour	65 Sqn	12	D9485	Capt H A Whistler	80 Sqn	6
D8118	Capt J Gilmour	65 Sqn	11	B2411	Various	65 Sqn	5
D1898	Capt O M Baldwin	73 Sqn	10	B3376	Capt E T Hayne	203 Sqn	5
D1929	Capt A H Cobby	4 AFC Sqn	10	B3756	Capt N W Webb	70 Sqn	5
B6202	Lt W A Curtis (7)	210 Sqn	9	B5598	Various	70 Sqn	5
B6340	F/Cdr R J O Compston	8 (N) Sqn	9	B6300	Capt A M Shook (4)	4 (N) Sqn	5
B6426	Lt F Gorringe	70 Sqn	9	B7199	Capt S T Edwards	209 Sqn	5
D9153	Various	46 Sqn	9	B9211	Capt C J Marchant	46 Sqn	5
F5941	Lt G B Gates	201 Sqn	9	C61	Capt R M Foster	209 Sqn	5
B6210	Capt J Trollope	43 Sqn	8	C1619	Capt T S Sharpe	73 Sqn	5
B5612	Capt J Gilmour	65 Sqn	8	C1627	Capt G E Thompson	46 Sqn	5
C6730	Capt D J Bell	3 Sqn	8	C1670	Capt J Todd	70 Sqn	5
C74	Capt C R R Hickey	204 Sqn	8	C8217	Various	70 Sqn	5
C8296	Lt W S Stephenson	73 Sqn	8	C8268	Lt F T Liversedge	70 Sqn	5
D1599	Lt D A Davies	150 Sqn	8	D1895	Lt R King	4 AFC Sqn	5
E1416	Capt A H Cobby (6)	4 AFC Sqn	8	D3354	Various	204 Sqn	5
B2447	Capt F G Quigley	70 Sqn	7	D9492	Capt G Graham	73 Sqn	5
C1615	Capt D J Bell	3 Sqn	7	D9599	Capt W R May	209 Sqn	5
D1911	Various	28 Sqn	7	D9618	Capt L H Rochford	203 Sqn	5
D8112	Lt C M McEwen	28 Sqn	7	E1407	Lt L E Taplin	4 AFC Sqn	5
E4407	Lt W S Jenkins	210 Sqn	7	E7160	Capt E J K McCloughry	4 AFC Sqn	5
E7279	Capt M A Newnham	65 Sqn	7	E7173	Lt K B Watson	70 Sqn	5
F3930	Capt K R Unger	210 Sqn	7	F2141	Lt H Burdick, USAS	17th Aero Sqn	5
B6363	Various	28 Sqn	6	F2328	Lt C F Pineau	210 Sqn	5
C66	Capt S J B Tonks (5)	204 Sqn	6	H7007	Various	65 Sqn	5
C197 L	Lt W Sidebottom	203 Sqn	6	N6376	F/Lt H T Mellings	10 (N) Sqn	5
				N6378	Capt R A Little	8 (N) Sqn	5

CAMEL 'ACES'

The following pilots claimed at least five victories flying Camels during the period 1917-19. The first column gives each pilot's actual Camel victories, while the second (bracketed) figure is the pilot's final war total.

Capt	D R McLaren	54	(54)	Capt J Cottle	12	(12)
Maj	W G Barker	41+	(52)	Lt G L Graham	12	(12)
Maj	J Gilmour	36	(40)	Capt F E Kindley, USAS	12	(12)
Capt	W L Jordan	34	(34)	Capt J G Manuel	12	(12)
Capt	F G Quigley	34	(34)	Capt A J B Tonks	12	(12)
Capt	A H Cobby	32	(32)	Maj A W Carter	11	(22)
Capt	H W Woollett	30	(36)	Capt H T Mellings	11	(15)
Capt	C M McEwen	27	(27)	Capt W H Hubbard	11	(12)
Capt	L H Rochford	26	(28)	Lt L T E Taplin	11	(12)
Capt	S M Kinkead	25	(40)	Capt W M Carlaw	11	(11)
Maj	R Collishaw	24	(62)	Lt D A Davies	11	(11)
Capt	J S T Fall	23	(36)	Capt O A P Heron	11	(11)
Capt	H A Whistler	23	(23)	Capt J E L Hunter	11	(11)
Capt	J L M White	22	(22)	Capt S T Liversedge	11	(11)
Capt	E J Kingston-McCloughry	21	(25)	Capt E J Lussier	11	(11)
Capt	G E Thompson	21	(23)	Capt J Mitchell	11	(11)
Capt	P Carpenter	21	(21)	Lt C W Payton	11	(11)
Capt	C R R Hickey	21	(21)	Capt G W Price	11	(11)
Capt	R King	20	(27)	Lt I C Sanderson	11	(11)
Capt	A T Whealey	20	(27)	Lt K R Unger	11	(11)
Capt	M B Frew	20	(26)	Lt A G Vlasto	11	(11)
Capt	C E Howell	19	(19)	Capt N W W Webb	10	(13)
Capt	D J Bell	18	(21)	Capt J D Breakey	10	(10)
Capt	C F King	18	(20)	Capt H C Daniel	10	(10)
Capt	C F Collett	18	(18)	Lt G S Hodson	10	(10)
Capt	M A Newnham	17	(17)	Capt W Hubbard	10	(10)
Capt	E Swale	17	(17)	Lt H B Hudson	10	(10)
Maj	R J O Compston	16	(26)	Lt E G Johnstone	10	(10)
Capt	O M Baldwin	16	(16)	Capt C J Marchant	10	(10)
Capt	M H Findlay	16	(16)	Capt H N C Robinson	10	(10)
Capt	H K Goode	16	(16)	FSLt H F Stackard	10	(10)
Capt	J A Greene	16	(16)	Capt W S Stephenson	10	(10)
Capt	G C MacKay	16	(16)	Capt T M Williams	10	(10)
Capt	J W Pinder	16	(16)	Capt R A Little	9	(47)
Capt	J Todd	16	(16)	Capt J A Glen	9	(16)
Capt	J L Trollope	16	(16)	Capt A R Brown	9	(13)
Capt	T F Williams	16	(16)	Capt H F Beamish	9	(12)
Capt	C P Brown	15	(15)	Capt C C Banks	9	(11)
Capt	G B Gates	15	(15)	Capt L H Slatter	9	(10)
Capt	E T Hayne	15	(15)	Lt G F M Apps	9	(9)
Capt	O W Redgate	15	(15)	Capt H B Bell	9	(9)
Capt	L P Coombes	14	(14)	Capt F J S Britnell	9	(9)
Capt	S C Joseph	14	(14)	Lt H R Clay, USAS	9	(9)
Capt	R McKierstead	14	(14)	Capt R J Dawes	9	(9)
Capt	A J Enstone	13	(18)	Capt M M Freehill	9	(9)
Capt	C G Bell	13	(13)	Lt R M Gordon	9	(9)
F/Cdr	W A Curtis	13	(13)	Lt L A Hamilton, USAS	9	(9)
Capt	S T Edwards	13	(13)	Capt F H Hobson	9	(9)
Capt	F C Gorringe	13	(13)	Capt M R James	9	(9)
Capt	G R Howsam	13	(13)	Capt C M Maud	9	(9)
Capt	W R May	13	(13)	Capt H A Patey	9	(9)
Lt	W Sidebottom	13	(13)	Capt J de C Paynter	9	(9)
Capt	S Stanger	13	(13)	Lt G R Riley	9	(9)
Capt	F S Symondson	13	(13)	Capt S P Smith	9	(9)
Capt	H G Watson	13	(13)	Capt W M Alexander	8	(19)
Capt	J B White	13	(13)	Capt F C Armstrong	8	(15)
Lt	G A Birks	12	(12)	Capt E W Springs, USAS	8	(12)
Capt	R C B Brading	12	(12)	Capt N Macmillan	8	(11)

Maj	H H Balfour	8	(10)
Capt	J C B Frith	8	(10)
Capt	G H Hackwill	8	(10)
Capt	P Wilson	8	(10)
Lt	G G Bailey	8	(8)
Capt	R J Brownell	8	(8)
Lt	W B Craig	8	(8)
Lt	J O Creech, USAS	8	(8)
F/Lt	H Day	8	(8)
Lt	A B Ellwood	8	(8)
Lt	H R Eycott-Martin	8	(8)
Lt	D S Ingalls, USN	8	(8)
Lt	A Jerrard, VC	8	(8)
Capt	N C Jones	8	(8)
Lt	W M MacDonald	8	(8)
Capt	G F Malley	8	(8)
Lt	C M Masters	8	(8)
Lt	H B Maund	8	(8)
Capt	T W Nash	8	(8)
Lt	J H Smith	8	(8)
Lt	M S Taylor	8	(8)
Capt	H le R Wallace	8	(8)
Capt	K B Montgomery	7	(12)
F/Cdr	C B Ridley	7	(9)
Lt-Col	J A Cunningham	7	(8)
Capt	J H Forman	7	(8)
Capt	C P Allen	7	(7)
Lt	A Buchanan	7	(7)
Lt	H Burdick, USAS	7	(7)
Lt	R G D'A Gifford	7	(7)
Capt	E McN Hand	7	(7)
Capt	W C Hilborn	7	(7)
Capt	J E Hallonquist	7	(7)
Lt	A L Jones	7	(7)
Capt	G Jones	7	(7)
Capt	W J MacKenzie	7	(7)
Capt	J Mackereth	7	(7)
Lt	C McEvoy	7	(7)
Capt	H M Moody	7	(7)
Lt	A E Robertson	7	(7)
Lt	C J Sims	7	(7)
Capt	J K Summers	7	(7)
Lt	K B Watson	7	(7)
Maj	C D Booker	6	(35+)
Capt	A M Shook	6	(13)
Lt	G A Vaughan, USAS	6	(13)
Capt	F M Kitto	6	(10)
F/Lt	N M MacGregor	6	(8)
Capt	J W Aldred	6	(7)
Maj	R Graham	6	(7)
Maj	M Le Blanc-Smith	6	(7)
Lt	K A Seth-Smith	6	(7)
Lt	E A L Smith	6	(7)
Lt	N C Trescowthick	6	(7)
Capt	C L Bissell, USAS	6	(6)
Lt	E B Booth	6	(6)
Lt	P Boulton	6	(6)
Lt	R N Chandler	6	(6)
Lt	H G Clappison	6	(6)
Lt	A G Cooper	6	(6)
Lt	G K Cooper	6	(6)
Lt	N Cooper	6	(6)
Lt	P M Dennett	6	(6)
Lt	J H Dewhurst	6	(6)
Lt	E C Eaton	6	(6)
Lt	A W Franklyn	6	(6)
Capt	G M D Gossip	6	(6)
Lt	A J Haines	6	(6)
Capt	W G R Hinchcliffe	6	(6)
Capt	D J Hughes	6	(6)
Lt	H C Knotts, USAS	6	(6)
Lt	A Koch	6	(6)
Capt	A A Leitch	6	(6)
Lt	G A Lingham	6	(6)
Lt	R K McConnell	6	(6)
Lt	C F Pineau	6	(6)
Capt	T S Sharpe	6	(6)
Lt	H C Smith	6	(6)
Capt	R Sykes	6	(6)
Capt	H L Symons	6	(6)
Capt	W D Tipton, USAS	6	(6)
Lt	A H Hunter	6	(6)
Lt	V M Yeates	6	(6)
Capt	T C R Baker	5	(11)
Maj	C J Q Brand	5	(11)
Capt	O C Le Boutillier	5	(8)
Capt	G A H Pidcock	5	(6)
Capt	D V Armstrong	5	(5)
Capt	M H Aten	5	(5)
Lt	A F Bartlett	5	(5)
Lt	G Brembridge	5	(5)
Capt	E G Brookes	5	(5)
F/Lt	W H Chisham	5	(5)
Capt	G M Cox	5	(5)
Capt	R C Crowden	5	(5)
Lt	H G W Debenham	5	(5)
Lt	C G Edwards	5	(5)
Capt	E Gribbon	5	(5)
Lt	M G Howell	5	(5)
Lt	A G Jarvis	5	(5)
Capt	F H Laurence	5	(5)
Lt	J D Lightbody	5	(5)
Lt	J S McDonald	5	(5)
Maj	R B Munday	5	(5)
Lt	O J Orr	5	(5)
Lt	R J Owen	5	(5)
Lt	A Paget	5	(5)
Lt	E H Peverell	5	(5)
F/Lt	E Pierce	5	(5)
Lt	O A Ralston, USAS	5	(5)
Lt	A Rice-Oxley	5	(5)
Lt	R M Todd	5	(5)
Lt	P M Tudhope	5	(5)
Capt	L E Whitehead	5	(5)
Lt	R D Williams, USAS	5	(5)

Thus, the above-named 231 Camel pilots were credited with a total of 2,425 confirmed victories in Camels alone. Additionally, the following fighter 'aces' included several Camel victories in their war totals, as indicated:

Capt	E D Crundall	4	(12)	Capt	W A Wright	3	(9)
Maj	A M Vaucour	4	(11)	F/Lt	D F Fitzgibbon	3	(8)
Capt	F J W Mellersh	4	(9)	Capt	H J T Saint	3	(8)
Capt	A H Orlebar	4	(9)	FSLt	G W Heming	3	(7)
Capt	J W Alcock	4	(7)	Capt	E Y Hughes	3	(6)
Lt	T H Barkell	4	(7)	Capt	M E Gonne	3	(5)
Capt	H H Maddocks	4	(7)	Capt	C W Odell	3	(5)
Maj	R S Maxwell	4	(7)	Maj	R S Dallas	3	(51)
Capt	P W S Bulman	4	(6)	Lt	A G A Spence	2	(8)
F/Lt	B P H De Roeper	4	(5)	Lt	A J Pallister	2	(7)
Capt	R P Minifie	3	(21)	FSLt	S E Ellis	2	(5)
Capt	A G Jones-Williams	3	(13)	Maj	A T Harris	2	(5)
Capt	A S G Lee	3	(11)	Lt	L A Callaghan, USAS	2	(5)
Maj	L S Breadner	3	(10)	Maj	G W Murlis-Green	1	(10)
Capt	St C C Taylor	3	(9)				

B6266, an unarmed training machine, in pristine servicing condition.

FLYING AND FIGHTING THE SOPWITH CAMEL

In 1918 student Camel pilots were issued with the following notes:

1. a. Always wear a belt or harness when flying the Sopwith Camel as there is a tendency to leave the seat when driving vertically.

    b. Do not turn to the right under 1,000 feet until you know the machine thoroughly, as the nose has a tendency to go down and lead you into a spin. In a vertically banked turn to the right, use left or top rudder, to keep nose up. In a similar turn to the left you require a good deal of left or bottom rudder to keep the nose down.

    c. When landing it is best to bring the machine down in calm weather at about 70 mph. gradually reducing speed as you near the ground. In windy or gusty weather it is better to land faster than this.

    d. Do not 'buzz' your engine whilst doing 'S' bends near the ground. If you put your engine on whilst doing a right hand turn, you are liable to side-slip and nosedive to earth, or to stall on a left hand turn.

    e. Learn when coming down from a height, to get over the aerodrome at about 1,000 feet and then land in the aerodrome without the help of your engine. It is the only way to learn to make forced landings successful. If you must 'buzz' your engine when coming into an aerodrome it is best to cut down throttle and fine adjustment to not over 1,000 revs before doing so.

    f. Do not forget to run your engine from your gravity tank from time to time. This is invaluable if your pressure tank is holed by 'Archie', or the pressure falls from some other cause.

    g. In a strong wind do not attempt to taxi in until you have men on both wing tips.

2. Learn to manoeuvre with a purpose — that of bringing your guns to bear on the hostile machine without him being able to fire at you. Practise the following:

    a. A quick change to an entirely opposite direction by vertically banked or stall turns. This is useful in diving on to an EA, especially a two-seater approaching in an opposite direction. Also used to throw an EA off your tail.

    b. A spin. To do this, shut off the engine and put the machine on a bank, kick on bottom rudder and pull in the stick. To come out of it, push stick forward and take off rudder. This manoeuvre is useful in losing height quickly to attack a machine much below you, or in throwing an EA off your tail. In the latter case do not go into a spin unless other methods such as a stall turn fail, as a spin always means loss of height.

    c. Vertical dives. Learn to shoot whilst diving as steeply as possible. You can practise this both on the range and by taking a sight through the Aldis on any ground object and diving as steeply as possible on to it. It is best to do this by shutting off petrol — leaving throttle and fine adjustments where they can give normal revs — and turn on petrol again at the bottom of the dive, or by shutting throttle *completely* until dive is finished. A vertical dive is most likely to surprise the EA you are attacking and offers him a poor target.

    d. A roll. To do this, get the machine going at about 70 mph, nose slightly up at an angle of about 30 degrees from the ground. Shut off engine. Pull stick back sharply and almost simultaneously kick on full rudder. Take off rudder when upside down and you will come butter-side up in normal flying position. The war value of this manoeuvre is not great but it might be used to impress an EA when attacking and to offer a poor target.

    e. Looping. Put the machine down to about 90 mph. Pull the stick back and take off right rudder. When over the vertical, cut off engine and pull the stick right back. This manoeuvre has been used successfully to throw an EA off the tail and bringing the attacked machine into a position of attack on the tail of an EA.

    f. Take every opportunity to practise 'scrapping' with another machine.

3.   Remember:

    a.   It is no good being able to out-manoeuvre a Hun unless you can shoot him down when your guns are brought to bear on him. Therefore practise at every opportunity on the range, and learn by the Deflector Teacher how to place the machine in the Aldis Sight.

    b.   That surprise is the first factor of success in aerial fighting and ability to out-manoeuvre your opponent the second. Therefore aim to get the sun behind you and when attacking. Height means speed, so keep as much height as possible before and during a scrap. A right hand Immelmann or stall turn in with the engine kept on until speed of dive becomes excessive is one method of throwing a Hun off your tail and getting onto his.

    c.   That you are vulnerable from the rear. Keep looking over your shoulder from time to time.

    d.   That a quick recognition of enemy aeroplanes is a great help in all aerial warfare. Study the official silhouettes.

    e.   That a pilot who is also a good observer is a very valuable and rare combination. Therefore train yourself to observe things on the ground as well as in the air and make out clear and concise reports. When new to the squadron, learn the position of all aerodromes and advanced landing grounds on this side in case of engine failure, and on the other side of the lines so that you know where to look for Huns.

FORMATION FLYING ON SOPWITH CAMEL

1.   Engines will be run punctually at half-an-hour before the formation is due at the lines, stopped, and any minor adjustments made. Twenty minutes before machines are due at the lines, all engines will be restarted and machines will get off as quickly as possible after the leader. BE PUNCTUAL.

2.   The leader will circle round the aerodrome at from 2,000 — 5,000 feet according to the height of the clouds until all machines are in their correct positions.

3.   The ground signal K will be put out or a red Very Light fired directly all machines are safely off the ground. The leader will understand from this signal that he may leave for the lines directly all machines are in formation. The ground signal W will indicate that he must continue to circle the aerodrome.

4.   Try and leave the ground as soon as possible after your leader, also to pick up formation without delay. Watch to see whether he is making right or left circuits and cut across to a point a mile of more ahead of him immediately on leaving the ground.

5.   If you are overshooting on an inside turn, throttle down or shut off your engine and dive and climb continuously in a vertical plane. Do NOT S-turn in a horizontal plane.

6.   Follow your leader. If he should dive on hostile machines, endeavour to follow him down as closely as possible so as not to lose formation. It is criminal to break formation in order to attack Huns. Act when your leader acts, but NOT before.

7.   Before a fight there are only two reasons which justify you in leaving the formation — (a) a failing engine, (b) both guns jammed.

8.   If your engine drops revs whilst you are in formation and some distance over the lines, it is much safer to fly *under* the formation even if you are several thousand feet below them than to straggle behind on the same level.

The partly-restored and spuriously serialled 'H508' when it was part of the Nash Collection of vintage aircraft and vehicles.

B5157, a veteran Camel which saw active service as 'M' of 210 Squadron in France, and was later doped overall in white at the Gosport School of Special Flying. Seen here at Gosport.

Appendix 10

DITCHING OF CAMELS

In the summer of 1918 a series of experiments with hydrovanes and flotation gear was undertaken at the Isle of Grain; with DH6, Curtiss JN4, FE2b and Sopwith 1½ Strutter aircraft all being ditched in a succession of trials. In mid-July a report stated that designs were being made of an improved flotation gear for Camels. In late July/early August a Camel (reported as '6341') was ditched in order to determine the type of gear needed. The machine was then salvaged and repaired and its engine overhauled. On August 9th another Camel, B3878 with a nine-inch steel hydrovane unit built in the front axle and a negative tail hydroplane on a long tail skid was deliberately ditched. The Camel landed on the water smoothly but immediately tipped onto its nose and began to sink; its tail hydrovane being ineffective. In late August an official report on ditchings was issued:

'REPORT ECD 120 – CAMEL HYDROVANES

A successful trail was made, using a six-inch wooden hydrovane built out in front of the wheels, as on a DH4. A pair of smaller wheels (450mm x 60) were fitted. Wind 15 mph. A good landing was made and the machine practically stopped before sinking down. There was no tendency to turn over on the nose.

The smaller wheels were fitted to decrease the resistance on touching the water. On service the smaller wheels would only be used when the machine was to be landed on the deck or in the water, the standard wheels being used for landing on aerodromes. The propeller clearance is decreased so that the tail guide on shipboard will have to be lower. Two blocks are fitted under the hydrovane to prevent the propeller touching the deck. Messrs Armstrong of Newcastle have been asked to forward their design of orientable deck for a barge to the Administrator, Works and Buildings at the earliest possible date for criticism, together with an estimate of the time and cost involved in its manufacture (a) with an 80 feet beam, (b) with a 50 feet beam. In view of the draft of this barge a being only 18-inches, this estimate is required for comparison with suggestions made recently to fit up barges loaned from the Admiralty with arresting gears.'

After this, two Camels were reported under post-ditching repair during September. In the course of this month a Camel was ditched with a wooden hydrovane, having jettisoned its wheels before landing. The machine, flying into a 15 mph wind, planed on to the water and sank gently without nosing up. An official summary of these ditching trials followed:

'SUMMARY OF REPORTS ON DITCHING EXPERIMENTS WITH CAMELS

First landing. From this experiment it was obvious that even with a slow landing the machine turned on its nose very violently and with considerable danger to the pilot. Some form of hydrovane must be fitted to prevent machine turning over on touching the water. Machine seriously damaged.

Second landing. Machine turned on its nose violently as when no hydrovane fitted, therefore hydrovane was designed, as on DH4, as far in front of the axle as propeller allowed. Also, small wheels were fitted to lessen resistance in water.

Third landing. This experiment was with the built-out hydro-vane and small wheels. As the landing was very slow and there was a 15 mph wind, it was considered necessary to land machine in a calm — this was done.

Fourth landing. As a result of this experiment it was thought necessary to improve the gear if possible. This was done by fitting dropping gear to the standard wheels, the wheels being held in place by a pin — when this pin is withdrawn a powerful spring shoots the wheel off. The wheels were dropped independently.

Fifth landing. This landing was entirely successful so that the gear is now considered satisfactory.

CONCLUSIONS: The gear is now considered quite satisfactory for the purpose, and neither pilot nor machine should be harmed by landing in a moderately calm sea.

The total weight (added), including fuselage airbags, is 27½ lb, and the added head resistance is small, so that there should be little deterioration of performance. (Performance tests will be made on a Clerget Camel with and without the gear). The wheel-dropping gear is simple in action and should be quite reliable.

No alteration has been made in the standard fuselage airbags for flotation as these have been found adequate in service.'

Another major project in relation to Camels being operated over the sea was the experimentation in towing single Camels on small, wood-topped lighters behind cruisers or other Fleet vessels in deep water. Pioneer of this particular form of seaborne operations was the veteran naval pilot, Commander Charles Rumney Samson, DSO; who by August 1918 was commander of No. 4 Group,, RAF. The original concept of lighter-borne aircraft belonged properly to Squadron Commander J C Porte in September 1916; but Samson was the first to experiment (personally) with Camels in this role, in May 1918. By the end of July successful take-off had been accomplished by Lieutenant Stuart Culley. Accordingly, the dynamic Samson immediately penned a memorandum, dated August 2nd, 1918, on the potential uses of Camels flown from towing lighters; which is reproduced here verbatim:

'SUGGESTED USES FOR CAMELS FLYING OFF TOWED LIGHTERS

(a)   Zeppelin daylight attacks.

The latest Zeppelins in commission have a ceiling of 20-22,000 ft. The service ceiling of a BR1 Camel is about 18,000 ft. Therefore, on occasions Zeppelins may escape but it is extremely likely that surprise attacks may be made. Zeppelins in daytime in the North Sea fly about 10-13,000 ft when on patrol near the Doggerbank Lightships.

If on days when the weather conditions are good, a destroyer could tow a lighter with a Camel aboard, arriving at the South Doggerbank Light Vessel at dawn, and remain cruising in the vicinity, sending up the Camel when the Zeppelin is sighted, it is certain that the Zeppelin will not see the Camel until the Zeppelin has got within 10 miles of the destroyer. The Camel would be given orders to climb to a higher altitude than the Zeppelin, keeping outside visual range from the Zeppelin i.e. about 7 miles or more for certainty and at the same time keeping to windward of the Zeppelin.

The Camel would take about 22-23 minutes to get to 15,000 feet and would then attack. The first warning the Zeppelin would get would be when the Camel was within 1-2 miles of it, as the Camel coming with the wind would be flying at 100-plus (say) 20 miles for wind — 120 miles an hour. Therefore, its approach would be at the rate of 2 miles a minute. Provided average shooting and no jams, the Zeppelins would have in my opinion, little chance to escape, especially so if the Camel kept its hiehgt until the last moment. The Camel could then return to the destroyer, come down into the sea, and the pilot would be picked up by the destroyer. The average time a Camel floats (from experience) is 3-5 minutes. On occasions with fairly empty tanks and a very good landing it would float longer.

Although I have fitted the Lighter with a powerful derrick I doubt if the Camel could be salved, but on occasions this would be possible.

A second destroyer would be required following the towing-destroyer — the whole operation would take about one hour.

(b)   Reconnaissance work and attacks on German seaplanes and mine-sweepers.

A single Camel would be of use for reconnaissance, but it is rather wasteful as the Camel will probably be lost after completing the reconnaissance; and the range cannot be relied upon to be more than 180 miles, being single seaters, and not capable of carrying much additional load. W/T could not be relied upon although some Camels have been so fitted.

For fighting German seaplanes, 3 or 4 Camels sent off from lighters at Terschelling Bank Light Vessel could reach eastern end of Ameland and return to destroyers close to the Haaks Light Vessel; the Haaks being much easier to pick up then a destroyer in the vicinity of Terschelling.

F2A's from Yarmouth or Felixstowe could work in conjunction with the Camels. The Camels only being sent up when the F2A's had sighted the Hostile aircraft.

The Camels could worry German minesweepers and destroyers to a great extent with machine guns and also by carrying 2-16lb bombs.

Camels attacking at 50-100 feet would be very difficult to deal with. I will keep one Camel ready and a Towing Lighter fitted with a flying deck. If a signal is made to me, I can always have the Camel and Flying Deck Lighter ready 3 hours after receipt of signal. I have demanded materials to fit decks on two more lighters. I have also asked for more Camels for this work. I have plenty of pilots in this Group, RAF who are very keen to fly Camels from Lighters on service.'

This memorandum was then endorsed in Samson's hand as follows:

'To Lieut Culley.

The part I have marked with pencil lines (para (a) above) refers to the method of carrying out the attack, you *must strictly carry out* this otherwise there is a chance of the Zeppelin outclimbing you. If you follow the rules you are certain to bring her down.

Aug 5th, 1918.'

Also attached to the original memorandum, in Samson's own hand, was a sheet of detailed instructions, as follows:

'The positions to avoid in a Zeppelin are (A) directly below or (B) behind its tail and below, unless in position B you can get in a blind spot. The best attack is a dive on top of it and then passing along just on its beam so as to avoid the flames. You should bag him in the first burst of shooting, especially if he puts up his nose to climb.

If you fail from this method, dive from behind him but on his quarter, but you will then be under heavy fire. Don't use all your ammunition in the first attack. Remember, according to our information the gun on top of the envelope is not used. Get close to the Zep; but keep out of danger of his flames, which will burst up pretty high; but mostly to leeward of the Zep, so you are alright (sic) if you keep ahead and on the bow.'

As related in the main text, Stuart Culley put his instructions to good effect in the main, taking off successfully and then destroying the airship L.53 on August 11th, 1918.

Appendix 11.

PILOTS' REPORTS ON THE GUARDIAN ANGEL PARACHUTE HARNESS

'I flew a Camel, wearing a Guardian Angel parachute harness, and found that those movements of my body which would be required when fighting were restricted, and that on turning my head to look backwards and downwards, my chin came against the rings which go round the shoulders. The top part of the rings cut into my shoulders, causing me considerable discomfort, which was increased by any movement of the arm, such as that necessitated by altering the throttle and fine adjustment openings.

Orfordness, 18/10/18   *Signed: O. Stewart, Major, RAF.*

'I wore this harness over my flying coat and then my shoulder straps and belt over all, in a Camel, flew for about an hour. The harness was certainly not comfortable. It impeded my movements to some extent, but on an extreme movement of my body, the metal rings hurt my shoulders, and I am quite sure that a long flight in a scout, when the pilot would be continually turning round, the harness would become extremely uncomfortable — in fact, impossible.

During the flight one of my shoulder straps slipped down over my arm. This is because the straps and belt are over the harness, which means it cannot fit well, and the shoulder straps will always be liable to slip off.

Another defect is that when a pilot is about to jump out with the parachute, he must first release his shoulder straps and belt, and it is most likely that they would be caught in the harness.

It is my opinion that this harness would be very uncomfortable after a long flight over the lines, in fact many pilots would refuse to wear it. For long distance bombing machines, or any machine where the pilot would not have to do much fighting, this harness may be suitable, but I am sure that for scouts or fighters it is an unreasonable design. Of course, when a suitable harness is designed for scouts, the same will be preferable for other machines too.

Orfordness, 19/10/18   *Signed: R.M. Charley, Captain, RAF.*

Appendix 12.

EXAMPLES IN SERVICE USE

To list the full career of every Camel ever built is clearly a near-impossible task. Nevertheless, in the context of the intention of this book as a work of reference, the following tabulation of *selected* examples of Camels in operational (and other) use is offered to the archivist and photograph collector. Each individual Camel listed here is known positively to have served at some period with the unit designated, though — as will quickly be noted by the discerning reader — many served with several units at varying periods. Where an individual unit letter or number was applied to a Camel, this — where known — is given in brackets following the serial number; but it should be noted that even within a single squadron several different Camels often carried the same marking at differing times; due to normal attrition and/or re-equipment and replacement circumstances. Though probably the most detailed listing of Camel serials published to date, the tables below represent merely a selection from a much more comprehensive listing gathered by the author over many years of private research. This 'master' list is still far from complete, and additional information on other individual Camels would be welcomed by this author.

3 Sqn RFC/RAF: B2451 (G); B2491 (T); B2520; B5238; B5433; B5440; B5450; B6234 (A); B6295 (Z); B6442 (A); B7275 (P); B7303; B7399 (Z); B9159; B9161; B9244; B9277; B9297 (W); C1582 (C); C1609; C1615; C1631; C1698; C1691 (Z); C6727; C6730; C8333 (8); C8374 (G); D1835 (2); D6442 (A); D6477 (Y); D6519 (S); D6593 (6); D6615 (Y); D6627 (R & U); D6655 (1); D9443 (F); E1402; E5178; F2125 (S); F2153 (7); F2173 (U); F5938; F6032 (R); F6089 (Z); H801; H810; H827; H829; H6855.

28 Sqn RFC/RAF: B2303; B2362; B2430; B2448; B3754; B5169 (B); B5183; B5237; B5401 (E); B5622; B5638; B6251; B6344 (G); B6345 (F); B6356; B6363 (K); B6406; B6413; B7208; B7171; B7147; B7247; B7351; B7354; B7383; B9152; B9306; B9310 (D); C134; D1911; D8103; D8110; D8170; D8208; D8213; D8241; D8244; E1502; E1503; E1581; F1921 (C).

37 Sqn RFC/RAF: E5135; E5141 (6); F1385 (C).

43 Sqn RFC/RAF: B2323 (M); B2340; B2367; B2392; B2431; B2460; B2477; B2510 (A); B5593; B5620; B5630; B6208; B6210; B6365; B7288; B7297; B7305; B7349; B7356; B7386; B7388; B7439; C8208 (N); C8240; C8247; C8248; C8262; C8270; C8281; C8291; D1778; D1785 (Z); D1809; D1815; D1819; D1840; D1864; D1894; D1956; D6402 (S); D6404; D6452; D9450; D9500; E1467; F6087; F6150.

44 Sqn RFC/RAF: B2343; B2402; B3767; B3899 (6); B5401; B5402 (2); B9175 (5); B9277 (2); B9307; C1555; H5899 (6); H5877 (2).

45 Sqn RFC/RAF: B2311; B2321 (S); B2323; B2327; B2338; B2340; B2350; B2376 (E); B2379; B2407 (R); B2426; B2426; B2430 (B); B2446; B2470; B2494 (S); B3791; B3871; B3875; B3903; B3914; B3925 (L); B3929 (L); B4609 (F); B5152 (M); B5182 (G); B5238; B6205; B6233; B6236; B6238 (C); B6312 (H); B6354 (N); B6383 (A); B6412 (D); B7167 (S); B7381 (H); B6372; D8237 (D); D8238; D9412.

46 Sqn RFC/RAF: B2314; B2348; B2429; B2451; B2457; B2501; B2522; B4618; B5208; B5247; B5419; B5425; B5434; B5436; B6405; B9149; B9157; B9183; B9195; B9197 B9199; B9211; B9273; C1554; C1572; C1617; C1627; C1637; C1643; C1659; C1685; C6722; D6407; D6418; D6491; D6509; D6511; D6585; D6603; D6667; D6681; D6693; D9405; D9411; E5157; D2137; F2137; F6210; H802; H826 ('JLL')

E7234, a standard F.1 Camel, which had its upper wing tips doped white for reasons unknown.

Fighting instructor and his F.1 Camel.

54 Sqn RFC/RAF:	B2483; B5203; B5243; B5414; B5417; B5421; B5422; B6293; B6403; B7171; B7320 (P); B7407; B9143; B9193; B9273; B0279; B9281; B9315; C1566; C1568; C1573; C1601; C1609; C3360; C6703; C8336; D1797; D1945; D1946; D1948; D6479; D6494; D6511; D6517; D6569; D6575; D6621; D9381; D9401; D9437; D9567; E5174; E5175; F1986; F2144; F2160; F2176; F5968; F6149; F6326; H7262; H7283.
65 Sqn RFC/RAF:	B2394; B2408; B2411; B2413; B2416; B2418; B2441; B2458 (R); B2487 (E); B2489; B5221; B5222; B5587; B5600; B5612; B5621; B5632; B6289 (A); B6335; B7227 (C); B7306; B7347; B7744; B9166; C8250; C8256; C8257; C8264; C8272; C8278; C8280; C8291; D1784; D1791; D1807 (T); D1811; D1876; D1878; D1887; D1903; D1921; D1960; D6474; D6552; D6562; D6630; D8118 (S); D8145; D8158; D8160; D8172; D8193; D8204; D9404; E1415; E1470; E1487; E1549; E7160; E7193; E7277; E7279; F1542; F5942 (Z); F6343; F6355; H7001; H7288.
66 Sqn RFC/RAF:	B2433; B2475; B2514; B4606; B5173; B5190; B5220; B5402; B5648 (E); B6207; B6313; B6326 (H); B6413 (J); B7283; B7353 (L); B7358; B7387; B7389 (T); C46; C3290; D1913; D6640; D8101 (P); D8233; D9390; D9414; D9588 (O); E1496; E1577; E7209; F1923.
70 Sqn RFC/RAF:	B2303; B2307; B2311; B2341; B2349; B2361 (C); B2389; B2396; B2444; B2447; B2449; B2452; B2492; B2499; B2530; B3754; B3756; B3777; B3780; B3787; B3813; B3823; B3836; B3838; B3840; B3873; B3889; B3890; B3915; B4630; B5179; B5214; B5408; B5598; B5640; B6206; B6234; B6251; B6283; B6366; B6426; B7320 (P); B7396 (G); B741; B7475; B9269; C1581; C1595; C1670; C1672; C1700; C8201; C8205; C8212; C8217; C8220; C8234; C8238; C8239; C8274; D1930; D3406; D6502; D6564; D6696; D9416; D9418; D9458; E1472; E1540 (D); E7162 (R); E7173; E7176; E7201; E7205 (F); E7241 (Z); E7277 (8); E7290 (H); F1933 (E); F2010 (5); F3995 (C).
71 Sqn RFC (4 AFC Sqn)	B778; B2387; B2409; B2424; B2448; B2474; B2488; B2489; B2520; B2527; B2531; B2535; B3903; B5208; B5217; B5585; B5602; B5625; B5629; B5635; B5644; B5649; B7180; B7347; B7382; B7385; B7390; B7406 (W); B7411 (Y); B7480; C3324; C8261; C8300; D1818; D1838; D1863; D1874; D1884; D1895; D1901; D1909; D1920; D1924; D1927; D1929; D1943; D1961; D6506; D6512; D6520; D6580; D6600; D6632; D8116; D8159; D8195; D8231; D9426; D9468; E1407; E1482; E1505; E1592; E7160; E7162 (R); E7180; E7190; E7202; E7233; E7241; F1403; F1415; F1548; F5948.
73 Sqn RFC/RAF:	B2351; B2473; B5449; B5568; B5572; B5590; B5627; B7282; B7292; B7302; B7322; B7867; B7874; B9261; C1619; C3312; C6723; C6733; C8269; C8292; C8296; D1776; D1783; D1794; D1812; D1841; D1898; D1918; D1922; D1958; D6484; D6504; D6572; D8106; D8164; D8199; D8202; D9448; D9448; D9382; D9398; D9478; D9480; D9498; E1551; E1553; E7184; F1540; F1917; F5920; F6063; F6107; F6351.
78 Sqn RFC/RAF:	B3752; B9287; B9309; C1555; D6401; D9459.
80 Sqn RAF:	B2463; B5154; B7292; B7322; B7346; B7434; B9132; B9170; B9209; B9235; B9293; B9323; B9325; C1581; C1623; C1647; C1699; C8203; C8205; C8254; D1789; D1849; D6457; D6481; D6505; D6591; D9429; D9485; F1968; F5927; F6110; F6151; F6251; H773.
112 Sqn RFC/RAF:	C6748; C8349; D6405; D6415; D6473; D6664; E5153; F1369; F2091; F4175.
150 Sqn RAF: (C Flt only)	C1586; C1587; C1598; D6549; D6551.
151 Sqn RAF:	B2504; B2517; B3852; B5412; B9301; C1629; C6713; C6717; C6725; C6753; C8227; C8229; D3357; D6405; D6423; D6568; D6573; D6651; D6652; D6660; D6673; D6682; D9441; D9445; D9501; D9572; D9577; E5142; F1887; F1970; F1979; F6084; F6088; F6090; F6102.

152 Sqn RAF: B2402; B5446; C6702; C6744; C6748; C853; D6465; D6603; D6673 D8164; D9445; D9465. E5142; E5148; E5164; E5168; F1311; F1323; F1379 F1381; F1884; F1890; F1891; F1961; F1991; F2149; F2152; F6084; F6090 F6111; F6122; F6370; F6376; H742.

1 (N) RNAS/ 201 Sqn RAF: N6330; N6371; N6379; B3882; B3884; B3919; B2921; B3950; B5748; B6211; B6203; B6204; B6211; B6244; B6258 (A); B6259; B6299; B6359 B6398; B6409; B6427; B6431; B7190; B7225; B7233; B7233; B7248; B7280 B7968; C64; C125 (H); C191; C196; C6718; D3363; D3393; D3419; D6431 (D) D6434; D6528; D9586; D9589; D9642; D9667 (B); D9669 (B); D9673; E4379; E4411; F3921 (C); F5227 (F); F5918; F5941 (E); F5991; F6022 (S); F6225; F6240; F6250; F6264.

3 (N) RNAS/ 203 Sqn RAF: B2442 (O); B3786; B3799; B3805; B3808; B3855; B3936; B5687 B6212; B6257; B6319; B6378; B6401; B7125; B7163; B7185; B7192; B7197; B7198; B7203; B7220; B7223; B7228; B7230; B7231; B7273; B7275; B7277; C197; D3370; D3376; D3384; D3413; D3417; D9581; D9585; D9592; D9611; D9618; D9624; D9632; D9640; D9651; D9671; F3933; N6364.

4 (N) Sqn RNAS/ 204 Sqn RAF: B3795; B3841; B3853; B3867; B3879; B3892; B3894; B3934; B6300 B6350. B6389; B7176; B7228; B7234; B7254; B7860; B8187; C66; C71; C72; C74; C75; C76; D1824; D1868; D3332; D3342; D3354; D3355; D3374; D3389; D3394; D3400; D8146; D8187; D8222; D9498; D9600; D9622; E4418; F3100; F3240; F3922; F3929; F6037; F8501; F8509; F9509; N6337; N6345.

6 (N) Sqn RNAS: B3821; B3833; B3835; B3882; B3883; B3919; B6228; B6311; B6318; B6340; B6356; B6379; B6447 ('SUSAN'); D1813; D1873; E7165; E7177 F5188; N6334; N6339; N6341; N6351; N6355; N6356; N6358; N6359; N6360; N6371; N6373; N6379.

8 (N) Sqn RNAS/ 208 Sqn RAF: B3759; B3773; B3794; B3785; B3819; B3821; B3845; B3853; B3868; B3921; B3922; B3939; B6227; B6260; B6311; B6319; B6321; B6340 (P); B6356; B6371; B6379; B7189; B7192; B7193; B7196; B7201; B7203; B7256; D1832; D1813; D1852; D1867; D1875; D1889; D1906; D1928; D1955; D3330; D3330; D3335; D3339; D3352; E1404; E1408; E1538; E1546; E1588; N6340; N6342; N6378.

9 (N) Sqn RNAS/ 209 Sqn RAF: B3810; B3818; B3819; B3820; B3830; B3832; B3858; B3869; B3880; B3883; B3892; B3893; B3897; B3905; B3906; B3919; B5651; B5664; B5749; B6204; B6217; B6230; B6356; B6358; B6369; B6389; B6398; B7190; B7199; B7200; B7233; B7245; B7247; B7249; B7250; B7270; B7272; B7471; C58; C51; C193; C198; C1585; D1891; D3326; D3328; D3329; D3332; D3340; D3345; D3351; D3373; D9599; D9607; D9621; D9636; E4380; E4389; E4393; F3225; F3233; F5925; F5944; F9657; H6997; N6356; N6370.

10 (N) Sqn RNAS/ 210 Sqn RAF: B2321 (5); B2490; B3808; B3817 (A); B3833; B3869; B3882; B3910; B3919; B3921; B3925 (L); B3940; B3950; B5152 (M); B5157 (M); B5658; B5663; B5664; B5749; B6201; B6202; B6204; B6211; B6225; B6242; B6244; B6289 (A); B6299 (B); B6330; B6342; B6355; B6358; B6449; B7153 (X); B7190; B7190; B7202; B7249; B7280; C62; C144; C200; D1872; D1883; D3332; D3350; D3364; D3381; D3390; D3399; D3410; D8219; D9499; D9548; D9590; D9600; D9613; D9622; D9626; D9631; D9675; E1405; E4383; E4390; E4405; E4421; F3106; F3132; F3930; F5914 (S); F5930; F6257; F8503; F8509; N6330; N6341; N6347; N6354; N6357; N659; N6376.

12 (N) Sqn RNAS/ 212 Sqn RAF: B3759; B3834; B3882; B3897; B3905; B5551; B5666; B6259; B6297; B6317; B6369; B6387; N6357; N6372.

13 (N) Sqn RNAS/ 213 Sqn RAF: B3773; B3774; B3782; B3793; B3909; B3936; B6202; B6240; B6400; B6407; B7175; B7186; B7226; B7254; B7270; B7272; B7274; C65; C66; C200; D3341; D3346; D3351; D3378; D3409; D8177; D8217; D9490; D9649; D9677; E1406; F3130; F3239; F3944 (6); F8504; F8508; F8511 (G); N6348; N6363.

220 Sqn RAF:	B5679; B6254; B7210; C51; D1970; D1971; D6612; D8138; D8140; D8142; D8155; N6804; N6805.
226 Sqn RAF: (Taranto)	C4; D6610; D6614; F6302.
227 Sqn RAF:	C43; C53; C133.
D Sqn RNAS: (Stavros)	B2442; B2543; B5680; B5682; B5690; B5728; B6438; B7207; B7212; C41; C49; C138; C140; D1966; D1969; N6367; N6352.
F Sqn RNAS: (Mudros)	B5676; B6255; B6353; B6367; B7182; B7207; D8155; F1951; F1952; N6353.
RNAS, Marsh:	B2543; B7182; D8139.
Malta:	D1949; D1950; N6806; N6806; N6807; N6808 (last three on HMS Manxman, based at Malta).
17th Aero Sqn, USAS:	B5428; B7407; B7896; B9166; B9268; C141; C1627; C3351; C8337; C8297; D1938; D1940; D1941; D3396; D6513; D6595; D9399; D9423; D9513; F1958; F1964; F2141; F2146; F2157; F2164; F5951; F5967; F5985; F5993; F6024; F6034; F6138; F6194; F6211; F6249; H828; H830; H7272; H7281.
41st Aero Sqn USAS:	C3283; C3291; C3295; C3303; C3339; C3352; F1431; F1432; F1434; F1445; F1452; F1473; F1485; F1490; F1502; F1517; F1521; H7235; H7280.
148th Aero Sqn, USAS:	B7329; B7349; B7359; B7869; B8155; B8216; C3302; C3307; C3308; C3310; C3343; C3353; C8201; C8253; C8255; D6546; D6574; D6700; D8165; D8166; D8171; D8180; D8195; D8196; D8203; D8245; D8246; D8249; D8250; D9516; D9519; D9555; E1412; E1414; E1470; E1471; E1479; E1506; E1530; E1539 (B); E1546; E1550; E1559; E1580; E1586 (S); E1588; E1594; E7192; E7231; E7239; E7243; E7290; E7291; E7329; E7330; F1400; F1414; F1478; F1546; F1550; F1934; F3943; F3949; F5191; F5943; F5945; F5946; F5948; F5983; F6058; F6135; F6169; F6175; F6176; F6185; F6191; F6194; F6201; F6253; F6353; F6383; F8508; F8553; H7359; H7389.
185th Aero Sqn, USAS:	C3305; C3309; C3321; C3329; C3346; C3350; C3352; C3354; C3358; F1430; F1437; F1440; F1445; F1449; F1455; F1464; F1476; F1488; F1490; F1498; F1499; F1511; F1517.
RNAS War School, Manston:	B3761; B3774; B3798; B3819; B3834; B3843; B3844; B3846; B3868; B3883; B3898; B3925; B5551; B5661; B5688; B5734; B6203; B6217; B6225; B6291; B6328; B7470; N6610; N6625; N6634.
204 TDS, Eastchurch:	B5576; B5713; B5719; B6280; B6281; C62; C1614; D1812; E1520; E1523; E1524; E1550; F4193; F4199; F4200; F4201; F9579.
63 TS, Joyce Green:	B2435; B4632; B7414; B7464; B7791; B7745; B7820; B7821; B8921; C130.
10 TS, Gosport:	B5215; B7316; B7359 (P); B9232 (V); B9316 (Q); C9 (P).
CFS, Upavon:	B3901; F9695; H8264; H8291; H8292.
5 (AFC) TS, Minchinhampton:	B2515; B5614; B5615; B5617; B5618; B5619; B6433; B9150; B9152; B9154; B9156; B9158; B9164; C101; C104; C106; C110; C122; C127; E1496; E1509; E5164; E7259; E7269; E7270; F1334; F1335; F1339; F1343; F1946.
6 & 8 TS (AFC), Leighterton:	B2315; B2515; B6432; B6433; B6436; B6442; B9162; B9248; C106; C121; C123; C127; E5165; E7267; E7287; F1347.
RNAS Donibristle:	N6602; N6607; N6637; N6641; N6751; N6842; N7100; N7125; N7128.

ABBEVILLE	91	EAST HAM	88
ABU SUEIR	143	EASTLEIGH	36,51
ALLONSVILLE	27	EGNA	49
ALBERT	30	ERINGHAM	32
AMERICUS	141	ESCAILLON	34
AMIENS	21,27	ESQUERDES	32
ANDRANA	123	ESTREES	91
ARCHANGEL	135	ESTREES-en-CHAUSEE	94
ASIAGO	38,42,45	ETREUX	94
ASOLA	57	FARNBOROUGH	143
ASTICO	45	FAUCOURT	34
AUCHEL	15	FELIXSTOWE	117
AUXI-le-CHATEAU	30	FELTRE	47,57
AVELIN	34	FIENVILLERS	15,32
BAIZIEUX	30	FLETRE	94
BANCOURT	94	FLEZ	21
BAPAUME	30,91,94	FOLKESTONE	86
BEKESBOURNE	86	FONTAINE-sur-MAYE	32,88
BELLEVUE	32	FOSSAMERLO	57
BERGUES	32	GALLIO	49,57
BERTANGLES	32	GERA	57
BEVERLEY	21	GHENT	125
BISSEGHEM	125	GHERTERLE	42
BOISDINGHEM	21	GHIRANO	38,41
BORDEAUX	141	GHISTELLES	36
BOURLON	94	GLIKI	120,123
BOURLON WOOD	30	GODEGA	57
BRAY DUNES	21	GORGO al MONTICO	41
BROOKLANDS	13,133	GRAINE (ISLE of)	105,117
BRUAY	21	GROSSA	38,57
BRUGES	24,30	GUANTANAMO	139
CAMBRAI	94	GUIA	47
CAMISANO	57	GUIZANCOURT	91
CAMPOFORMIDO	49	GULLANE	94
CANDAS	21	HAIDA PASHA	123
CAPORETTO	38	HAINAULT FARM	83,88
CAPELLE	27,32	HAMPTON ROADS	139,141
CAPPY	34	HARTY FERRY	88
CASARSA	42	HELIGOLAND BIGHT	112
CASTELLO di CODEGA	51	HENDON	143
CHOISY-le-ROI	139	HEULE	125
CONEGLIANO	51,57	HORNCHURCH	86
CONSTANTINOPE	123	IMBROS	120,123
CORNARE	57	ISTRANA	38
COURTRAI	36	KALLONI	120
DETLING	86	KASSANDRA	123
DORIGNIES	32	KELLY FIELD	141
DOULLENS	27,30	KOIVISTO	117
DOVER	18,36,83	LA GORGUE	24
DRAMA	123	LA LOVIE	18
DROGLANDT	15,54	LAKE GARDA	49
DUNKIRK	13,15,21,27	LAKEDOWN	36
DURRAZZO	123	LANGLEY FIELD	139,141

*   *   *   *

PHOTO CREDITS/ACKNOWLEDGEMENTS

A proportion of the photographs used in this book were made available to me by the unselfish generosity of several eminent aviation historians and many other good friends and acquaintances. The list below is my personal credit for the *sources* of these photos, and should not be misinterpreted as inferring any legal claim to any copyright necessarily. On this latter point, it may be as well to point out that, under the Copyright Act of 1956, all such photos are now (strictly speaking) in 'free public domain' — i.e. out of copyright protection; a legal point still unrecognised or misunderstood by many present-day institutions and holders of 'original' prints and/or negatives. Nevertheless, I have attempted to establish legal copyright in each case, and therefore the ultimate responsibility for any legal 'infringement' is mine alone. To the following, listed alphabetically, I owe a continuing debt of deep gratitude:

Squadron Leader R.C.B. Ashworth, RAF; Captain J. Brown, R.N. Ret'd; Flight Lieutenant R.A. Brown, RAF; J.M. Bruce, MA, FRHistS, AMRAeS; R. Buck; late Air Vice-Marshal R. Collishaw, CB, DSO, OBE, DSC, DFC; Wing Commander E.D. Crundall, DFC, AFC; J.B. Cynk; Major C. Draper, N.L.R. Franks, Esq; E. Gee Esq; B.T. Gibbins, Esq; E.A. Harlin, Esq; A. Imrie, Esq; late Flight Lieutenant A. Jerrard, VC; P. Kilduff, Esq; late Colonel Y.E.S. Kirkpatrick; Group Captain G.M. Knocker, RAF Ret'd; G. Stuart Leslie, Esq; D.G. Lewis, Esq; J.T.C. Long, Esq, Esq; C.J. Marchant, Dr. S.Z. Ross; late H.H. Russell, Esq; R.L. Sargent, Esq; C. Schaedel, Esq; F.T.S. Sehl, Esq; F. Selinger, Esq; R.C. Shelley, Esq; Captain R. Sykes, DFC; Lt-Colonel Avi M. Terlinden, BEM; Mrs A.C. Harington nee Tilbury; R. Vann, Esq; W.J. Wales, Esq; Squadron Leader D.W. Warne, RAF; A.C. Watts, Esq; Wing Commander F.W. Weatherill; G.H. Williams, Esq; H. Woodman; H. Hugh Wynne, Esq; F. Yeoman, Esq.

In addition the following sources provided certain photographs:

31 Squadron Association; 43 Squadron Association; Public Archives of Canada; Royal Canadian Air Force; Hawker Siddeley Aviation Co., Kingston-upon-Thames; Imperial War Museum; Ministry of Defence (Air); AELR Air Museum, Brussels; Australian War Memorial; the Winthorpe Collection.

© 1978. CHAZ BOWYER

ISBN 0 9502825 7 X

Published by Glasney Press, 28A High Street, Falmouth.

Produced by Oxford Print Consultants
8 The Roundway, Headington, Oxford.

They Gave Their Today
A Book of Heroes

A Forgotten Veterans UK Publication

All proceeds from the sale of this book go directly to supporting Service Veterans in need around the UK

www.forgottenveteransuk.com
Registered Charity No: 1175556

Editor In Chief:

Peter Macey

Co-Editor:

Christina Drummond

Editorial Team:

Angie O'Carroll
Douglas Miller
Thomas Fairley
Gary Weaving
Catherine Macey
Mark Mason

Cover Design:

Glyn Macey

Printer:

David Willis, Wm. Anderson & Sons Limited, Glasgow

Photographs:

Special thanks to Ellie Taylor for the extract from her book, 'Faith, Hope & Rice', detailing the experiences of her veteran father, Fred, and used with the kind permission of Pen & Sword Books.

Memories Page – Thank you to all who submitted articles.

ISBN: 978-1-9164965-1-4

9 781916 496514

First Edition Print 75 copies – May 2019